SCHOLASTIC

Teaching
Vocabulary Words
With Multiple Meanings

Rebecca Lamb

New York • Toronto • London • Auckland • Sydney
Mexico City • New Delhi • Hong Kong • Buenos Aires

Teaching *Resources*

◎ ACKNOWLEDGEMENTS ◎

There are many people who helped make this book a reality. First, I would like to thank my colleagues at Overlook Elementary School in Linthicum, Maryland for embracing this idea from the beginning and for providing quality feedback for how to improve the material. They also offered ideas for additional words and activities to include. While many helped move this project from an idea to the printed page, I am compelled to mention the names of some who provided the greatest amount of input and support to the project:

- Betty Freeland, principal—for her initial support of the idea and for promoting the idea of publishing the project.

- Patie Kneisly, gifted/talented resource teacher—for helping brainstorm the concept, conducting research, proofreading, and editing.

- Lenora Fox, Colleen McFarland, Zetta Hart and Beth Burke, resource teachers—for their friendship and support in suggesting and drafting activities, and for willingly proofreading anything I gave them.

- Karen Schmidt and Lori Ginsberg, teachers—for their creative ideas in brainstorming activities and for trying them with their students.

- Ruth Bowman and Kim Callison, Coordinators of Reading/Language Arts—for their support and encouragement.

Finally, I would be remiss if I did not acknowledge my family. This book would not be possible without their love and support. Marty's devotion and skillful editing and computer skills, my mother's meticulous proofreading, and Jeremy and Owen's patience kept the process moving. They provided the time and encouragement I needed to make a dream a reality.

Edited and produced by Immacula A. Rhodes

Cover design by Ka-Yeon Kim

Interior illustrations by Teresa Anderko

Interior design by Sydney Wright

ISBN-13: 978-0-545-05402-7

ISBN-10: 0-545-05402-8

◎ Contents ◎

Introduction

Students frequently encounter words with multiple meanings—or *polysemy*—in their daily activities. Conversations, directions, and reading materials are often laced with words such as *back*, *file*, *play*, and *set*, which require understanding of the various definitions of these words to make sense of them. In addition, the vocabulary section of many standardized tests include polysemous words. While reading the words during test-taking is rarely a problem, students often stumble over unfamiliar question formats and the confusion posed by the multiple definitions of these words. That's where the vocabulary-enhancement activities in *Teaching Vocabulary Words With Multiple Meanings* can help.

This book is designed to be a launching pad for exploring and discussing polysemous words. The activities are formatted to help students systematically work with a different word each week to reinforce its various meanings. And since they take only minutes a day to do, the exercises can easily be integrated into your language arts curriculum.

Through explicit instruction and rich discussions, you can use the activities with students to build vocabulary and comprehension skills, reinforce writing and critical thinking skills, boost confidence in word usage, and teach effective strategies for understanding, using, and working with multiple-meaning words. In addition to daily vocabulary instruction, the activities are great for use with students who are learning English as a second language and for providing struggling readers with extra practice.

The activities in *Teaching Vocabulary Words With Multiple Meanings* are effective for typical classroom use, but they can be implemented in a variety of other ways as well. For example, a school-wide "Word of the Week" activity might be established to introduce and reinforce a targeted multiple-meaning word in morning announcements or the school newsletter. In addition, the featured word might be displayed on a hallway bulletin board that invites students to add to the display as they discover examples of the word in various forms of print (such as magazines and newspapers) and in illustrations. Students might also create and add their own sentences and art illustrating the diverse meanings of the word.

Why Teach About Words With Multiple Meanings?

A quick look in any dictionary will reveal that most words in the English language have more than one meaning. In fact, the more frequently a word is used, the more meanings it is likely to have (Miller & Gildea, 1987). Many words have a primary meaning, and one or more somewhat obscure secondary meanings. But there are also a considerable number of words for which several meanings are used often and fairly equally. When students encounter these words, they need to be familiar with the different meanings and uses of them.

Multiple-meaning words like *grade* (see box at left) can confuse students and derail their comprehension of an entire passage. Mixing these meanings can make

Many words have several meanings. For example, definitions for *grade* include:

- a level in school
- a score on a test
- to check or give a score to an assignment
- a measure of quality
- to make something more level
- the slope of a road or incline

reading frustrating: Is the passage talking about the quality of a piece of meat, or how well someone did on a test? Word meanings are inherently flexible, and always nuanced in some way by the context in which they occur. The meaning of a word must be inferred from context, even if the word is already familiar.

Five key areas of reading instruction were identified by the National Reading Panel (2000): phonemic awareness, phonics, fluency, vocabulary, and comprehension. This book focuses on the vocabulary component that is essential for reading success. As illustrated with the word *grade*, comprehension often relies on the understanding of vocabulary. Developing a strong vocabulary not only boosts students' reading comprehension, but also helps them become more confident in word usage.

The Partnership for Reading (2003) notes that vocabulary instruction should focus on important, useful, and difficult words that have multiple meanings. The language arts standards outlined by Mid-continent Research for Education and Learning (McREL) state that students must be able to understand level-appropriate vocabulary including synonyms, antonyms, homophones, and multi-meaning words (Kendall et al., 1999). In addition, the *Standards for the English Language Arts* (National Council of Teachers of English, 2008) recommends that students apply a wide range of strategies to comprehend texts by drawing on prior experience, knowledge of word meaning, and word identification skills. Since many of the multiple-meaning words in this book are used frequently and widely across content areas and grade levels, the activities can help strengthen students' vocabulary knowledge and reading comprehension across the content areas.

Why Provide Explicit Instruction?

According to Nilsen and Nilsen (2003), the "secret to teaching vocabulary is keeping students interested in a word long enough that their minds will have time to absorb the many possible meanings." Given this, teachers should consider introducing and working with only one word at a time to give students the time and opportunity to think about, explore, and really learn its definitions and usage. Beck, McKeown & Kucan (2002) suggest using student-friendly explanations to help students learn words, rather than relying on the often vague and confusing definitions found in dictionaries. In addition, Brabham & Villaume (2002) have found that word study is ineffective when students copy definitions.

Short, focused classroom discussion is the key to successful implementation of the activities in this book. It is through direct instruction, rich discussions, and teacher modeling that students develop understanding of polysemous words and learn strategies that help them demonstrate their knowledge of the words. While the obvious point of these activities is to teach multiple-meaning words, the deeper purpose is to get children to look at various possibilities and strategies for unlocking their diverse meanings. In addition to being familiar with its polysemy, knowledge of a word includes knowing how it sounds, how it is written, and how it is used as a part of speech (Juel & Deffes, 2004). Instruction with these activities includes using word knowledge and context clues, and also reinforces test-taking strategies.

One Word Is Not Equal to Another

Often, English language learners approach the language as if it were math or science by trying to equate one word precisely to another. The concept that one word can have more than one meaning doesn't make sense to these students, causing confusion when they encounter multiple-meaning words in text. In addition, they often try to spell the words differently in different contexts. This notion is further reinforced in that many words with identical pronunciations but different meanings—such as *no* and *know*—are spelled differently.

How to Use This Book

What's Inside?

Five reproducible activities are provided for each of the 50 feature words. You can copy the activities and cut them apart for use on an overhead projector or document camera, as well as for distribution to students. Keep in mind that the activities were created for explicit, direct instruction. Discussion is critical—the activities were not designed with independent student work in mind.

You can use the dictionary (pages 114–126) as a quick reference to find the different parts of speech for a particular word, as well as examples of its diverse meanings. While the list of meanings for a word is not comprehensive, you'll find a definition that matches each use of the word in the daily activities in addition to several frequently used meanings. Note that the dictionary is designed as a reference for your use. The pages should not be distributed to students to study or memorize word meanings. The goal of this book is not to have students memorize words or definitions, but rather to help them interact with these tricky words through explicit instruction and rich discussions.

Introducing Multiple-Meaning Words

Before doing the activities in this book, you might use lighthearted, humorous stories—such as those in Peggy Parish's *Amelia Bedelia* series—as a springboard for introducing multiple-meaning words. Amelia's misunderstandings provide amusing, but effective examples of how confusing some word meanings can be. For instance, when told to "dress the chicken," she makes overalls and a shirt for the bird to wear. Children enjoy pointing out Amelia's mix-ups and explaining the intended meaning of the polysemous words that confuse this delightful character. During read-alouds, you might pause to discuss the meanings of these tricky words, point out pictures that illustrate them, and use the words in a variety of ways to demonstrate one or more of their meanings.

Other books that help students explore multiple-meaning words include *Deputy Dan and the Bank Robbers* by Joseph Rosenbloom, *The King Who Rained* by Fred Gwynne, and the easy reader *See the Yak Yak* by Charles Ghigna. The text and illustrations in such books can help students begin to understand the complexities of polysemy as they encounter and discuss the confusion these words can cause.

Reinforcing Vocabulary

Playing with words and their meanings in activities such as those listed below enables students to develop a metacognitive understanding of how words work (Blachowicz & Fisher, 2004). These activities can also be used to assess student understanding of multiple-meaning words.

◎ Ask students to describe pictures or objects. Ask them to explain different definitions for words that have multiple meanings, such as *table* or *hand*.

◎ Invite students to search magazines to find pictures that illustrate various meanings of a word.

▲▽▲▽▲▽▲▽▲▽▲▽▲▽

Experience and Exposure Builds Vocabulary

The National Reading Panel concluded that vocabulary should be taught both directly by class activities and indirectly through student experiences. *Put Reading First* (2001) further states that repeated exposure to vocabulary in various contexts aids word learning. The more children encounter words the better they seem to learn them. In addition, the use of concrete materials for vocabulary development can be very motivating and effective. Students acquire more vocabulary and content information when they can touch and see the information (Rule and Barrera, 2003).

◎ Prepare definition or picture cards for students to use while playing charades or a modified game of Pictionary. Provide two or more versions of the same word, making a separate card for each version. As students take turns acting out or drawing clues, check for their understanding of the different meanings.

◎ Challenge students to write as many sentences as possible for a multiple-meaning word, using a different definition for each sentence.

◎ Create spider maps or word webs to record different meanings, sentences, pictures, and so on related to a targeted polysemous word.

Using the Activities

The pages for each word in *Teaching Vocabulary Words With Multiple Meanings* include a different activity for each of five days for you to use with students. To introduce the word, start with "Guess the Word!" Then, as you work through each daily activity with students, discuss the word and model "think aloud" strategies they might use to discover, explore, and determine how and where the word is used and its different definitions. It will only take 5–10 minutes a day to complete each activity with students.

The following is an example of how you might use each daily activity to teach about the word *play*. This demonstration suggests ways you might guide students in exploring and discussing the word and its meanings, as well as how you might model useful strategies to help them build confidence in their word knowledge and usage. You can follow this example, modifying it as necessary, to teach the daily activities for other words in the book.

Day 1: Guess the Word!

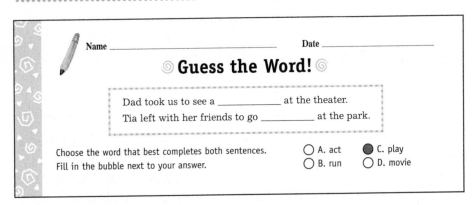

This introductory activity leads students to discover the word to be studied. Two sentences are shown in the box, with each containing a missing word. While the missing word in each sentence will be the same, each sentence uses the word in a different way. After students choose the word from the four answer choices that best completes both sentences, they fill in the bubble next to their answer.

1. Read aloud the first sentence, pausing at the blank to indicate that a word is missing. Read the four answer choices.

   • Have students test each word in the sentence. Discuss which words are the most plausible to complete the sentence and why. For instance, *play* and *movie* are the most reasonable choices for the first sentence.

- Help students understand why the remaining words don't work. Here, *act* could be a likely fit, but the use of *a* before the blank should signal that a word that begins with a vowel won't work.
- Ask students to share their reasoning about why a word does or does not work in the sentence.

2. Repeat step 1 for the second sentence. Help students understand that *act, run,* and *play* are all plausible answers. Guide them to discover that a verb is needed to complete the sentence. Since *movie* is a noun, it can be eliminated.

3. Read aloud both sentences once again, this time filling in the blank for one sentence with each reasonable word choice for the other sentence.
- Have students discuss each choice and why it does or does not work in both sentences. Is there one word that works equally well in both sentences?
- Ask students to fill in the bubble beside their choice.

4. Review the sentences and discuss the part of speech and meaning of *play* in the context of each sentence. (In the first sentence, *play* is a noun meaning "a story performed on stage"; in the second sentence, it is a verb meaning "to amuse oneself.")
- Invite students to share their prior knowledge about the word and its use as well as to ask any questions that come up.
- You might use information from the discussion to assess what students already know and additional information they need to learn about the word and its uses. For instance, students might need to learn that as a verb, *play* can also mean "to make sound or music" (as in *play a piano*) or "to take part in a game" (as in *play checkers*).

Day 2: Match a picture to the word meaning

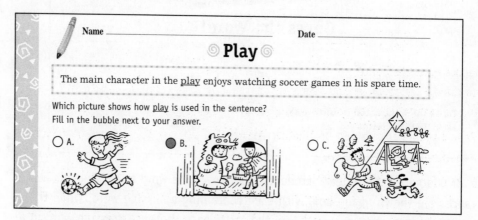

This activity includes a sentence with the targeted word underlined. Students examine the three picture choices under the sentence and decide which picture shows how the word is used in the sentence.

1. Read aloud the sentence and point out the underlined word (*play*). Help students determine the part of speech of the word—here, *play* is a noun.

2. Discuss each illustration and the meaning or meanings of *play* represented in it. Also, help students identify what part of speech *play* might be used as. For

example, *play* in A might be a noun meaning "a move in a game" or a verb meaning "to take part in a game." In B, it might be a noun meaning "a story performed on stage" or a verb meaning "to perform or do." In C, *play* is a verb meaning "to amuse oneself."

3. Guide students to select the correct picture (B, in this case) and to share reasons why the other choices are incorrect. For instance, while A shows a child playing soccer—and soccer is mentioned in the sentence—the use of *play* in the sentence refers to a story acted out on stage and not a move in a game.
   - Have students fill in the bubble beside their choice.
   - Ask students to make up sentences using *play* according to its meaning in the incorrect pictures.

4. Point out test-taking strategies that students might use to determine the correct answer. For example, they can eliminate C because *play* in that picture represents a different part of speech than is used for *play* in the sentence.

5. Include explorations of other meanings for the word. As new meanings are mentioned, have students make up sentences that use the word in that way.

Day 3: Choose the correct definition for the word

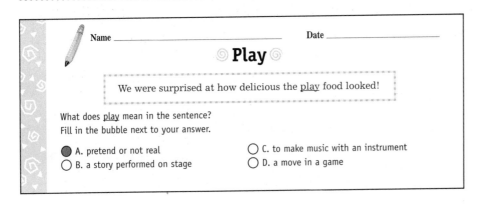

Students read the sentence in the box and choose the best definition for the underlined word from among four choices. In most cases, the four definitions are different meanings of the same word.

1. Read the sentence aloud and help students identify the part of speech for the underlined word (adjective).

2. Discuss each of the four definition choices.
   - Ask students to identify what part of speech each definition represents. Here, choice A is an adjective, B is a noun, C is a verb, and D is a noun.
   - To reinforce test-taking strategies, help students understand that they can eliminate any answer choices that represent a different part of speech than the one used in the sentence. Here, only A is a viable choice since it's the only definition for the adjective *play*.

3. Have students test the most likely choices by replacing the underlined word with the definition. For instance, they can reread the target sentence as "We were surprised at how delicious the *pretend or not real* food looked."

- Discuss the plausibility of each choice. At times, students may need to use higher level thinking skills and differentiate between subtle differences in word meanings as they do this activity.
- Have students fill in the bubble beside the best definition.

4. Ask students to brainstorm sentences with the other definitions of the word. You might use this activity to assess students' understanding of the various meanings.

Day 4: Use the word to write meaningful sentences

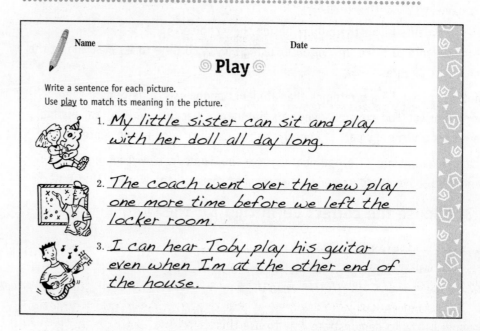

Name _____   Date _____

◎ Play ◎

Write a sentence for each picture.
Use play to match its meaning in the picture.

1. *My little sister can sit and play with her doll all day long.*

2. *The coach went over the new play one more time before we left the locker room.*

3. *I can hear Toby play his guitar even when I'm at the other end of the house.*

This activity encourages students to use what they know about the word and its meanings. They examine three pictures depicting a different meaning of the word and then write a sentence for each picture to demonstrate how the word is used.

1. Examine each picture and discuss the possible meanings of *play* as it is represented in the picture.

2. Help students decide which part of speech for *play* is most likely depicted in each picture. For instance, in 1, *play* is used as a verb meaning "to amuse oneself." It is a noun in 2, meaning "a move or action in a game," and a verb meaning "to make music" in 3.

3. Ask students to come up with a sentence to write beside each picture, using *play* in the same way it is meant in the picture.

- Have students check that they used the word as the same part of speech that is depicted in the picture. You might model how to check the word usage in one or two sentences that you create before having students complete the activity.

- When students understand how to do this activity, you might have them complete it for independent practice. You can then use the sentences to informally assess their understanding of the multiple meanings of a word.

Alternate Activity for Day 4:
Match the best definition to each profession

Name _____ Date _____

◎ Press ◎

> Press can mean:
> A. to iron wrinkles out of something
> B. to push or hold something down
> C. to squeeze juice from something
> D. newspapers and magazines

Find the definition of <u>press</u> that each person would most likely use.
Write the letter on the line.

B 1. elevator operator   *D* 4. politician

D 2. reporter   *C* 5. chef

A 3. seamstress   *A* 6. dry cleaner

For some words, the activity for Day 4 will follow the format shown here. In this activity, students decide which of several definitions is the one most likely used by each of the six professionals listed. The purpose is to encourage critical thinking about various word meanings. The activity for "Press" is used as an example below to demonstrate how to use this exercise to teach about the word.

1. Read aloud and discuss each definition in the box.

2. Read the name of each professional one at a time. Talk about what the professional does.

3. Use a think-aloud approach to model how students might decide which definition of *press* is most likely to be used by each professional.

   • For elevator operator, you might say, "I know that an elevator operator takes people up and down floors in a building. In his job, he most likely won't need to iron out wrinkles or squeeze juice from something, so I can rule out *A* and *C*. He might come across newspapers and magazines (as in *D*), but these don't relate to his job. But, he must push elevator buttons and sometimes hold them down while doing his job. The most logical choice for this profession is *B*."

   • Have students write the letter for their choice beside each professional.

4. Focus discussions on why certain professionals would more likely use one definition versus another. You might enhance students' vocabulary further by including additional descriptions of each professional's job, talking about items or equipment they use, and sharing other titles that might apply to the professional.

Day 5: Match the word usage in sentences

Name _____ Date _____

◎ Play ◎

> My brothers and I <u>play</u> stickball with our neighbors after school.

Which sentence uses <u>play</u> in the same way as the sentence in the box?
Fill in the bubble next to your answer.

○ A. The students asked if they could use puppets in their <u>play</u>.

○ B. My little sister uses <u>play</u> money when she takes pretend shopping trips.

○ C. I'm taking lessons to learn how to <u>play</u> the piano.

● D. At recess, our teacher likes to <u>play</u> soccer with the class.

This activity provides a target sentence with the feature word underlined and a set of four additional sentences that use the same word. Students read the sentences and then identify which of the four sentences uses the word in the same way as the target sentence.

1. Read aloud the target sentence. Discuss the meaning of the underlined word and its part of speech. In this example, *play* is a verb that means "to take part in a game."

2. Read each sentence choice. Repeat step 1 for *play* in each sentence. Help students identify context clues—such as specific words, definitions, examples, and comparisons—that might be useful in determining how the word is used. For example, in *A*, *puppets* might clue students that a show is involved. In *B*, *pretend shopping trip* suggests engaging in something that is not real, and *piano* in *C* suggests that music is involved. In *D*, soccer might signal that the word is related to a game.

3. Help students use the test-taking strategy of elimination to rule out implausible choices.

   • Have students fill in the bubble next to their answer. (In this activity, the correct answer is *D*.)

   • To further assess students' knowledge of the multiple meanings of *play*, challenge them to make up sentences that could be paired with the incorrect choices.

References and Resources

Anderson, R. C., & Nagy, W. E. (1991). Word meanings. In R. Barr, M. L. Kamil, P. B. Mosenthal, & P. D. Pearson (Eds.), *Handbook of reading research* (Vol. 2, pp. 690–724).

Armbruster, B. B., Lehr, F. & Osborn, J. (2001). *Put reading first: The research building blocks for teaching children to read.* Washington, DC: National Institute for Literacy and US Department of Education.

Beck, I. L., McKeown, M. G. & Kucan, L. (2002). *Bringing words to life: Robust vocabulary instruction.* New York: The Guilford Press.

Blachowicz, C. L. Z. & Fisher, P. (2004). Vocabulary lessons. *Educational Leadership*, 61(6), 66–69.

Brabham, E. G. & Villaume, S. K. (2002). Vocabulary instruction: Concerns and visions. *The Reading Teacher*, 56(3), 264–268.

Carlo, M. S., August, D., McLaughlin, B., Snow, C., et al. (2004). Closing the gap: Addressing the vocabulary needs of English-language learners in bilingual and mainstream classrooms. *Reading Research Quarterly*, 39(2), 188–215.

Ghigna, C. (1999). *See the Yak Yak.* New York: Random House.

Gwynne, F. (1988). *The King Who Rained.* New York: Aladdin.

Juel, C. & Deffes, R. (2004). Making words stick. *Educational Leadership*, 61(6), 30–34.

Kendall, J. S. & Marzano, R. J. (2004). *Content knowledge: A compendium of standards and benchmarks for K–12 education.* Aurora, CO: Mid-continent Research for Education and Learning. Online database: www.mcrel.org/standards-benchmarks

Kendall, J. S., Snyder, C. Schintgen, M., Wahlquist, A. & Marzano, R. J. (1999). *A distillation of subject-matter content for the subject areas of language arts, mathematics, and science.* Aurora, CO: Mid-continent Research for Education and Learning.

Miller, G. A. & Gildea, P. M. (1987). How children learn words. *Scientific American*, 257(3), 86–91.

National Council of Teachers of English (2008). *Standards for the English Language Arts.* Available online at: www.ncte.org/about/over/standards/110846.htm

National Reading Panel (2000). *Teaching children to read: An evidence-based assessment of the scientific research literature on reading and its implications for reading instruction.* Washington, DC: National Institute of Child Health and Human Development.

Nilsen, A. P. & Nilsen, D. L. F. (2003). A new spin on teaching vocabulary: A source-based approach. *The Reading Teacher*, 56(5), 436–439.

Parish, P. *Amelia Bedelia* series. New York: Scholastic.

Partnership for Reading (2003). *Bringing scientific evidence to learning: vocabulary instruction.* Available online at: www.nifl.gov/partnershipforreading/explore/vocabulary.html

Rosenbloom, J. (1985). *Deputy Dan and the bank robbers.* New York: Random House.

Rule, A. C. & Barrera, M. T. (2003). Using objects to teach vocabulary words with multiple meanings. *Montessori Life*, 15(3), 14–17.

Stahl, S. (1999). *Vocabulary development.* Cambridge, MA: Brookline Books.

Name _____ Date _____

◎ Guess the Word! ◎

Congress passed an _____ to help protect our country.

The second _____ of the play was funny and interesting.

Choose the word that best completes both sentences. ○ A. operate   ○ C. obey
Fill in the bubble next to your answer.   ○ B. act   ○ D. appeal

---

Name _____ Date _____

◎ Act ◎

Jim and Jodi <u>act</u> like kittens when they drink their milk.

Which picture shows how <u>act</u> is used in the sentence?
Fill in the bubble next to your answer.

○ A. ○ B.  ○ C.

Name _____ Date _____

◎ Act ◎

We had to <u>act</u> quickly to keep the flies out of the house.

What does <u>act</u> mean in the sentence?
Fill in the bubble next to your answer.

○ A. move or take action   ○ C. have an effect on something
○ B. pretend to be something else   ○ D. perform a role in a play or movie

◎ Act ◎

Write a sentence for each picture.
Use <u>act</u> to match its meaning in the picture.

1. _____
_____
_____

2. _____
_____
_____

3. _____
_____
_____

- -

Name _____   Date _____

◎ Act ◎

> Our teacher asked us to write a play and <u>act</u> it out for the class.

Which sentence uses <u>act</u> in the same way as the sentence in the box?
Fill in the bubble next to your answer.

○ A. If you <u>act</u> fast, you can still get to the play on time.

○ B. The main character sang two solos in the last <u>act</u> of the play.

○ C. Our group will <u>act</u> out *The Three Little Pigs* on Monday.

○ D. My younger sister began to <u>act</u> up in the middle of dinner.

Name _____ Date _____

◎ Guess the Word! ◎

I want to go _____ to the amusement park next summer.

Dad had to _____ the car out of the garage.

Choose the word that best completes both sentences.
Fill in the bubble next to your answer.

○ A. back ○ C. return
○ B. reverse ○ D. past

Name _____ Date _____

◎ Back ◎

Mrs. Perry patted John on the <u>back</u> for a job well done.

Which picture shows how <u>back</u> is used in the sentence?
Fill in the bubble next to your answer.

○ A. ○ B.  ○ C.

Name _____ Date _____

◎ Back ◎

Most voters <u>back</u> the plan for the new recreation center.

What does <u>back</u> mean in the sentence?
Fill in the bubble next to your answer.

○ A. to return to a place or condition ○ C. to support something
○ B. to move in reverse ○ D. to be behind at a distance

◎ Back ◎

Write a sentence for each picture.
Use <u>back</u> to match its meaning in the picture.

1. _____
   _____
   _____

2. _____
   _____
   _____

3. _____
   _____
   _____

- -

◎ Back ◎

> Mom told Jared to put the balls <u>back</u> in the shed.

Which sentence uses <u>back</u> in the same way as the sentence in the box?
Fill in the bubble next to your answer.

○ A. I showed how I solved the problems on the <u>back</u> of my test.

○ B. Dora hit the <u>back</u> of her head when she fell down the stairs.

○ C. Brian and Tommy ran out the <u>back</u> door.

○ D. The salesperson hung the clothes <u>back</u> on the rack.

◎ Guess the Word! ◎

George put a _____ around the papers to hold them together.

The _____ played *The Star Spangled Banner* before the game.

Choose the word that best completes both sentences.
Fill in the bubble next to your answer.

○ A. group   ○ C. band
○ B. string   ○ D. ring

◎ Band ◎

When Leah packed up her drums, she put a <u>band</u> around her drumsticks.

Which picture shows how <u>band</u> is used in the sentence?
Fill in the bubble next to your answer.

○ A.   ○ B.   ○ C.

◎ Band ◎

I wore a blue shirt with a white <u>band</u> around the middle.

What does <u>band</u> mean in the sentence?
Fill in the bubble next to your answer.

○ A. a stripe of color   ○ C. to gather or form in a group
○ B. a group of musicians   ○ D. a rubber loop used to hold things together

◎ Band ◎

Write a sentence for each picture.
Use <u>band</u> to match its meaning in the picture.

1. _____
   _____
   _____

2. _____
   _____
   _____

3. _____
   _____
   _____

Name _____   Date _____

◎ Band ◎

In the movie, a <u>band</u> of pirates divided the treasure in the chest.

Which sentence uses <u>band</u> in the same way as the sentence in the box?
Fill in the bubble next to your answer.

○ A. The papers scattered everywhere when the <u>band</u> around them broke.

○ B. We watched the <u>band</u> perform on the football field at halftime.

○ C. My sister lost her wedding <u>band</u> at the beach.

○ D. The sheriff promised to catch the <u>band</u> of mailbox thieves in our town.

◎ Guess the Word! ◎

She sat on the _____ of the river to fish.

I put all my coins in a piggy _____ on my shelf.

Choose the word that best completes both sentences.   ○ A. depend   ○ C. mound
Fill in the bubble next to your answer.   ○ B. edge   ○ D. bank

---

Name _____   Date _____

◎ Bank ◎

Sally went to the <u>bank</u> to deposit money into her savings account.

Which picture shows how <u>bank</u> is used in the sentence?
Fill in the bubble next to your answer.

○ A.    ○ B.    ○ C.

Name _____   Date _____

◎ Bank ◎

Fred knew he could <u>bank</u> on his friends to help him move.

What does <u>bank</u> mean in the sentence?
Fill in the bubble next to your answer.

○ A. a place where people deposit or   ○ C. depend on or be sure of something
withdraw money

○ B. a large mound or heap of something   ○ D. the ground alongside a river or lake

Name _____ Date _____

◎ Bank ◎

> Bank can mean:
>
> A. a place where people deposit or withdraw money
>
> B. a large mound or heap of something
>
> C. the ground alongside a river or lake
>
> D. to rely or depend on someone

Find the definition of bank that each person would most likely use.
Write the letter on the line.

_____ 1. political candidate   _____ 4. teller

_____ 2. boat pilot   _____ 5. snow ski instructor

_____ 3. dirt bike rider   _____ 6. water skier

Name _____ Date _____

◎ Bank ◎

> That bank of clouds looks like a fluffy teddy bear.

Which sentence uses bank in the same way as the sentence in the box?
Fill in the bubble next to your answer.

◯ A. The tour guide pointed out a large bank of snow along the road.

◯ B. My mother volunteers at the blood bank several times a year.

◯ C. Casey saves all of her quarters in a piggy bank.

◯ D. Mom cashed a check at the bank during her lunch break.

◎ Guess the Word! ◎

Sometimes, the sergeant has to ____ orders at the new soldiers.

Every time a truck passes, our Dalmatian begins to ____ wildly.

Choose the word that best completes both sentences.
Fill in the bubble next to your answer.

○ A. yell   ○ C. bark

○ B. screech   ○ D. pant

◎ Bark ◎

Some <u>bark</u> fell off the tree as the squirrel climbed up the trunk.

Which picture shows how <u>bark</u> is used in the sentence?
Fill in the bubble next to your answer.

○ A.    ○ B.    ○ C.

◎ Bark ◎

The fans could hear the coach <u>bark</u> instructions to the football players.

What does <u>bark</u> mean in the sentence?
Fill in the bubble next to your answer.

○ A. to speak loudly and sharply   ○ C. to whisper softly

○ B. the sound a dog makes   ○ D. to write in a secret code

Name _____ **Date** _____

⊚ Bark ⊚

> Bark can mean:
>
> A. the outer covering of a tree trunk
>
> B. the short, loud sound made by a dog, fox, or seal
>
> C. to speak loudly and sharply
>
> D. an old word for a large sailing ship

Find the definition of <u>bark</u> that each person would most likely use.
Write the letter on the line.

_____ 1. animal trainer   _____ 4. veterinarian

_____ 2. historian   _____ 5. military commander

_____ 3. park ranger   _____ 6. boat builder

Name _____ **Date** _____

⊚ Bark ⊚

> Dan's dog would <u>bark</u> loudly when the doorbell rang.

Which sentence uses <u>bark</u> in the same way as the sentence in the box?
Fill in the bubble next to your answer.

◯ A. We carved the <u>bark</u> off the logs to make smooth fence posts.

◯ B. An old-fashioned ship, or <u>bark</u>, was docked at the harbor.

◯ C. When the commander began to <u>bark</u> out orders, the troops moved quickly.

◯ D. I was surprised to hear two seals <u>bark</u> at each other.

Name _____ Date _____

◎ Guess the Word! ◎

The children used a _____ to break open the piñata.

A _____ sleeps during the day and hunts for food at night.

Choose the word that best completes both sentences.
Fill in the bubble next to your answer.

○ A. bat   ○ C. rod
○ B. stick   ○ D. club

Name _____ Date _____

◎ Bat ◎

The baseball player hit the ball into the outfield with a wooden <u>bat</u>.

Which picture shows how <u>bat</u> is used in the sentence?
Fill in the bubble next to your answer.

○ A.    ○ B.   ○ C.

Name _____ Date _____

◎ Bat ◎

The furry <u>bat</u> hung upside down in the dark cave.

What does <u>bat</u> mean in the sentence?
Fill in the bubble next to your answer.

○ A. a wooden stick or club   ○ C. a mammal that has wings and flies
○ B. to hit at something   ○ D. to take a turn at hitting in baseball

◎ Bat ◎

Write a sentence for each picture.
Use <u>bat</u> to match its meaning in the picture.

1. _____
   _____
   _____

2. _____
   _____
   _____

3. _____
   _____
   _____

◎ Bat ◎

> I hope I get a new baseball <u>bat</u> for my birthday.

Which sentence uses <u>bat</u> in the same way as the sentence in the box?
Fill in the bubble next to your answer.

◯ A. My friend wore a <u>bat</u> costume for Halloween.

◯ B. Ernesto hit a home run when it was his turn to <u>bat</u>.

◯ C. Cal's <u>bat</u> broke in two when he hit the ball.

◯ D. We saw the <u>bat</u> fly out of our neighbor's attic.

Name _____   Date _____

◎ Guess the Word! ◎

The bird caught the worm in its strong, sharp _____.

Mr. Jones frowned when he saw the _____ for his car repair.

Choose the word that best completes both sentences.
Fill in the bubble next to your answer.

○ A. beak   ○ C. bill
○ B. check   ○ D. law

Name _____   Date _____

◎ Bill ◎

I paid for our meal with a twenty-dollar <u>bill</u>.

Which picture shows how <u>bill</u> is used in the sentence?
Fill in the bubble next to your answer.

○ A.   ○ B.    ○ C.

Name _____   Date _____

◎ Bill ◎

The dentist will <u>bill</u> the insurance company for my visit today.

What does <u>bill</u> mean in the sentence?
Fill in the bubble next to your answer.

○ A. a piece of paper money

○ B. a poster or flyer that
advertises something

○ C. a list of charges for services or work done

○ D. to send a note showing how much
someone owes for something

Name _____ Date _____

◎ Bill ◎

Bill can mean:
A. a piece of paper money
B. the draft of a law being presented for approval
C. a bird's beak
D. a poster or flyer that advertises something

Find the definition of <u>bill</u> that each person would most likely use.
Write the letter on the line.

_____ 1. veterinarian   _____ 4. senator

_____ 2. car dealer   _____ 5. bird watcher

_____ 3. banker   _____ 6. treasurer

Name _____ Date _____

◎ Bill ◎

The phone <u>bill</u> for this month was higher than usual.

Which sentence uses <u>bill</u> in the same way as the sentence in the box?
Fill in the bubble next to your answer.

○ A. We saw a clown post a <u>bill</u> that advertised when the circus would be in town.

○ B. My dad wrote a check to pay the <u>bill</u> at the hotel.

○ C. Mom said the doctor would <u>bill</u> us for the x-rays of my broken arm.

○ D. My neighbor gave me a ten-dollar <u>bill</u> for helping him rake the leaves.

Name _____ Date _____

◎ Guess the Word! ◎

I want just a little _____ of sugar in my coffee.

The carpenter replaced the drill _____ before he drilled the hole.

Choose the word that best completes both sentences.
Fill in the bubble next to your answer.

○ A. part   ○ C. moment
○ B. piece   ○ D. bit

Name _____ Date _____

◎ Bit ◎

The horse jockey uses a bridle and <u>bit</u> to control her horse.

Which picture shows how <u>bit</u> is used in the sentence?
Fill in the bubble next to your answer.

○ A. 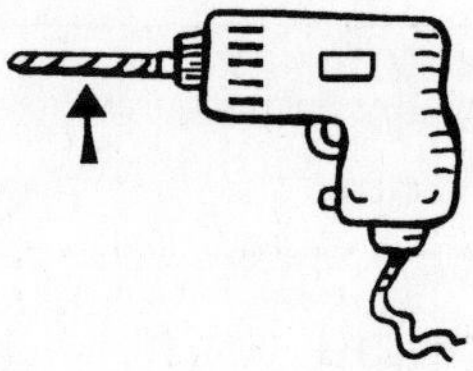   ○ B.    ○ C.

Name _____ Date _____

◎ Bit ◎

Mom called to say that she would be here in a <u>bit</u>.

What does <u>bit</u> mean in the sentence?
Fill in the bubble next to your answer.

○ A. a small piece or part   ○ C. the part of a drill used when making a hole
○ B. a short time   ○ D. the past tense of bite

◎ Bit ◎

Write a sentence for each picture.

Use <u>bit</u> to match its meaning in the picture.

1. _____
   _____
   _____

2. _____
   _____
   _____

3. _____
   _____
   _____

◎ Bit ◎

> When Kate finished her project, she had only a <u>bit</u> of glue left.

Which sentence uses <u>bit</u> in the same way as the sentence in the box?
Fill in the bubble next to your answer.

◯ A. Sam <u>bit</u> into the largest cookie in the batch.

◯ B. The horse refused to open its mouth to take the <u>bit</u>.

◯ C. We still have to wait a <u>bit</u> before we can go to lunch.

◯ D. Jane left a <u>bit</u> of bread on her plate.

◎ Guess the Word! ◎

We have a _____ of seats for the play so we can all sit together.

Jack put a curved _____ on top of the tall tower he built.

Choose the word that best completes both sentences.   ○ A. group   ○ C. block

Fill in the bubble next to your answer.   ○ B. row   ○ D. wood

---

◎ Block ◎

Our P.E. teacher jogs around the <u>block</u> every day for exercise.

Which picture shows how <u>block</u> is used in the sentence?

Fill in the bubble next to your answer.

○ A.   ○ B.   ○ C.

◎ Block ◎

I held the paper over my head to <u>block</u> the sun from my eyes.

What does <u>block</u> mean in the sentence?

Fill in the bubble next to your answer.

○ A. a batch or group of something

○ B. a city street

○ C. a plastic or wooden cube that children play with

○ D. an obstacle that prevents one thing from reaching another

◎ Block ◎

Write a sentence for each picture.
Use <u>block</u> to match its meaning in the picture.

1. _____
_____
_____

2. _____
_____
_____

3. _____
_____
_____

◎ Block ◎

> The police had to <u>block</u> the road while the wreck was cleared away.

Which sentence uses <u>block</u> in the same way as the sentence in the box?
Fill in the bubble next to your answer.

○ A. Mina bought a <u>block</u> of tickets for the show.

○ B. When I finished my homework, I took a walk around the <u>block</u>.

○ C. We stacked sandbags around the house to <u>block</u> the floodwaters.

○ D. Dad's new cutting board is a solid <u>block</u> of wood.

Name _____ Date _____

◎ Guess the Word! ◎

The class took a short _____ between the two tests.

We tried to _____ the record for collecting the most canned foods.

Choose the word that best completes both sentences.

Fill in the bubble next to your answer.

○ A. rest   ○ C. beat
○ B. break   ○ D. chance

Name _____ Date _____

◎ Break ◎

Tell the boys to <u>break</u> the cookie in two and share it.

Which picture shows how <u>break</u> is used in the sentence?

Fill in the bubble next to your answer.

○ A.   ○ B.    ○ C.

Name _____ Date _____

◎ Break ◎

The students made a <u>break</u> for the door when the last bell rang.

What does <u>break</u> mean in the sentence?

Fill in the bubble next to your answer.

○ A. to come apart or separate   ○ C. an opportunity
○ B. to rush away   ○ D. to stop working

Name _____ Date _____

◉ Break ◉

Write a sentence for each picture.
Use <u>break</u> to match its meaning in the picture.

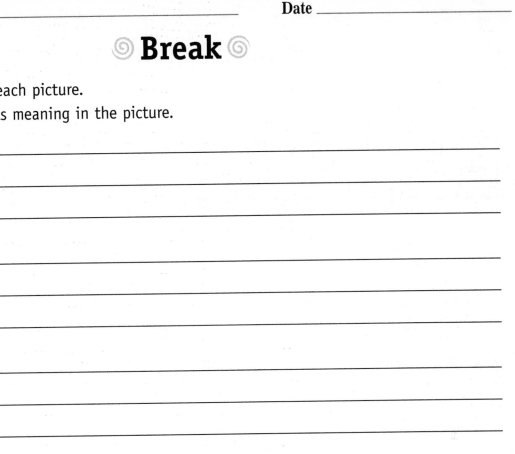

1. _____

_____

_____

2. _____

_____

_____

3. _____

_____

_____

Name _____ Date _____

◉ Break ◉

> Stephanie's big <u>break</u> came when she acted in *The Wizard of Oz*.

Which sentence uses <u>break</u> in the same way as the sentence in the box?
Fill in the bubble next to your answer.

○ A. Jenny is trying to <u>break</u> her nail-biting habit.

○ B. I helped my brother repair a <u>break</u> in the fence yesterday.

○ C. Cory made a <u>break</u> for the car when it started to rain.

○ D. I hope Joel will get the <u>break</u> he needs to become famous.

Teaching Vocabulary Words With Multiple Meanings © 2008 by Rebecca Lamb, Scholastic Teaching Resources, 33

Name _____ Date _____

◎ Guess the Word! ◎

The rabbit hopped into the _____ that grows beside the road.

I screamed when I felt something _____ against me in the dark house.

Choose the word that best completes both sentences.
Fill in the bubble next to your answer.

○ A. brush   ○ C. bush
○ B. sweep   ○ D. rub

Name _____ Date _____

◎ Brush ◎

The stylist used a round <u>brush</u> to curl Jill's hair.

Which picture shows how <u>brush</u> is used in the sentence?
Fill in the bubble next to your answer.

○ A.    ○ B.    ○ C.

Name _____ Date _____

◎ Brush ◎

The scouts had a <u>brush</u> with danger when they almost fell off the cliff.

What does <u>brush</u> mean in the sentence?
Fill in the bubble next to your answer.

○ A. to touch lightly in passing   ○ C. to sweep
○ B. an encounter   ○ D. to groom an animal with a tool that has bristles

◎ Brush ◎

Write a sentence for each picture.
Use <u>brush</u> to match its meaning in the picture.

1. _____
   _____
   _____

2. _____
   _____
   _____

3. _____
   _____
   _____

- -

◎ Brush ◎

> Mom tried to <u>brush</u> away the dust with her hand.

Which sentence uses <u>brush</u> in the same way as the sentence in the box?
Fill in the bubble next to your answer.

○ A. I use a special <u>brush</u> to get the tangles out of my horse's tail.

○ B. You can use this cloth to <u>brush</u> the snow off your coat.

○ C. If you <u>brush</u> against the thorny bushes, stickers might get on your clothes.

○ D. The dentist told me to <u>brush</u> my teeth twice a day.

◎ Guess the Word! ◎

We tried to get Gino to _____ his mind about buying those shoes.

I have less than a dollar of _____ in my pocket.

Choose the word that best completes both sentences.
Fill in the bubble next to your answer.

○ A. switch   ○ C. change
○ B. coins   ○ D. replace

Name _____   **Date** _____

◎ Change ◎

I always put my <u>change</u> in a big jug next to my bookshelf.

Which picture shows how <u>change</u> is used in the sentence?
Fill in the bubble next to your answer.

○ A.    ○ B. 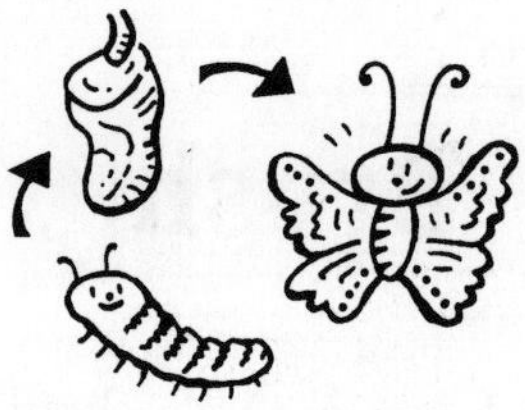   ○ C.

Name _____   **Date** _____

◎ Change ◎

My brother went home to <u>change</u> clothes for the game.

What does <u>change</u> mean in the sentence?
Fill in the bubble next to your answer.

○ A. to make or become different   ○ C. to give money back
○ B. to replace one thing with another   ○ D. to take turns

◎ Change ◎

Write a sentence for each picture.
Use change to match its meaning in the picture.

1. _____

_____

_____

2. _____

_____

_____

3. _____

_____

_____

◎ Change ◎

> I like to lie on the ground and watch the clouds change shapes.

Which sentence uses change in the same way as the sentence in the box?
Fill in the bubble next to your answer.

○ A. The tiny tadpoles will change into frogs soon.

○ B. I decided to change my answer to the question.

○ C. My sister asked if I had enough change to buy her a soda.

○ D. Our teacher told us to change seats with our neighbors.

Name _____   Date _____

◎ Guess the Word! ◎

Dale had to _____ the battery before he played his new game.

We watched the football players _____ toward the dropped ball.

Choose the word that best completes both sentences.
Fill in the bubble next to your answer.

○ A. play   ○ C. attack
○ B. rush   ○ D. charge

Name _____   Date _____

◎ Charge ◎

Our plan is to <u>charge</u> for the roller coaster as soon as the gates open.

Which picture shows how <u>charge</u> is used in the sentence?
Fill in the bubble next to your answer.

○ A.   ○ B.    ○ C.

Name _____   Date _____

◎ Charge ◎

What is the <u>charge</u> for a ticket to the amusement park?

What does <u>charge</u> mean in the sentence?
Fill in the bubble next to your answer.

○ A. the price for a thing or service   ○ C. to place the blame on someone
○ B. to put off paying for something until later   ○ D. to rush toward someone or something

◎ Charge ◎

Write a sentence for each picture.
Use charge to match its meaning in the picture.

1. _____
   _____
   _____

2. _____
   _____
   _____

3. _____
   _____
   _____

◎ Charge ◎

The bowling alley owner said she would charge us for only one pair of shoes.

Which sentence uses charge in the same way as the sentence in the box?
Fill in the bubble next to your answer.

○ A. It took three hours for Sarah to charge her remote-control car.

○ B. I am in charge of keeping the books in order on the shelves.

○ C. The hair stylist had to charge the lady for a shampoo and haircut.

○ D. Many people charge expensive TVs instead of paying cash for them.

◎ Guess the Word! ◎

My dad wrote a _____ to pay for my new shoes.

The waitress brought the _____ at the end of our meal.

Choose the word that best completes both sentences.
Fill in the bubble next to your answer.

○ A. check ○ C. ticket
○ B. bill ○ D. view

◎ Check ◎

The teacher marked a <u>check</u> next to all the correct answers.

Which picture shows how <u>check</u> is used in the sentence?
Fill in the bubble next to your answer.

○ A.　　　　　　○ B. ✓　　　　　　○ C.

◎ Check ◎

Please <u>check</u> the address before you mail that letter.

What does <u>check</u> mean in the sentence?
Fill in the bubble next to your answer.

○ A. to make sure something is correct
○ B. a mark used to indicate a correct answer
○ C. a pattern of squares
○ D. the bill at a restaurant

Teaching Vocabulary Words With Multiple Meanings © 2008 by Rebecca Lamb, Scholastic Teaching Resources, 40

Name _____ **Date** _____

◎ Check ◎

> Check can mean:
>
> A. to see if something is working right
>
> B. a mark used to indicate a correct answer
>
> C. a slip of paper directing the bank to pay a certain amount
>
> D. the bill at a restaurant

Find the definition of <u>check</u> that each person would most likely use.
Write the letter on the line.

_____ 1. waitress   _____ 4. teacher

_____ 2. mechanic   _____ 5. electrician

_____ 3. bank teller   _____ 6. professor

Name _____ **Date** _____

◎ Check ◎

> I wore my red <u>check</u> shirt on our field trip to the farm.

Which sentence uses <u>check</u> in the same way as the sentence in the box?
Fill in the bubble next to your answer.

○ A. The clerk asked the lady to show the claim <u>check</u> for her coat.

○ B. Will you <u>check</u> your bag to make sure you have a house key?

○ C. Mr. Lee paid the <u>check</u> for his daughter's birthday dinner.

○ D. Each <u>check</u> in the quilt is made of a different color.

Name _____ Date _____

◎ Guess the Word! ◎

My favorite _____ of the meal was dessert.

Aunt Pam is taking a computer _____ at the local college.

Choose the word that best completes both sentences.
Fill in the bubble next to your answer.

- ○ A. course
- ○ B. part
- ○ C. class
- ○ D. plan

Name _____ Date _____

◎ Course ◎

Tony said that his uncle's house was not far off our <u>course</u>.

Which picture shows how <u>course</u> is used in the sentence?
Fill in the bubble next to your answer.

○ A.    ○ B.   ○ C.

Name _____ Date _____

◎ Course ◎

Many followed Karen's <u>course</u> of action to clean up the community.

What does <u>course</u> mean in the sentence?
Fill in the bubble next to your answer.

- ○ A. a path or track
- ○ B. a class
- ○ C. part of a meal
- ○ D. a plan or procedure

Name _____ Date _____

◎ Course ◎

Course can mean:

A. one part of a meal

B. a class

C. a route or track used for certain sports

D. a plan or procedure

Find the definition of course that each person would most likely use.
Write the letter on the line.

_____ 1. professor   _____ 4. college student

_____ 2. pilot   _____ 5. waiter

_____ 3. chef   _____ 6. snow skier

Name _____ Date _____

◎ Course ◎

My uncle teaches a course on writing children's books.

Which sentence uses course in the same way as the sentence in the box?
Fill in the bubble next to your answer.

○ A. Of course, I will attend my sister's birthday party.

○ B. The driving course was lined with orange cones and barrels.

○ C. James believes that he is taking the hardest course in school.

○ D. The waiter took my plate before I was finished with the main course.

Name _____   Date _____

◎ Guess the Word! ◎

Gramps wrapped a _____ around his shoulders to keep warm.

Who wants to _____ the story about the food drive for our newspaper?

Choose the word that best completes both sentences.
Fill in the bubble next to your answer.

○ A. blanket   ○ C. write
○ B. cover   ○ D. protect

Name _____   Date _____

◎ Cover ◎

Amy uses a blanket to <u>cover</u> her sofa when the kids come over to play.

Which picture shows how <u>cover</u> is used in the sentence?
Fill in the bubble next to your answer.

○ A.   ○ B. 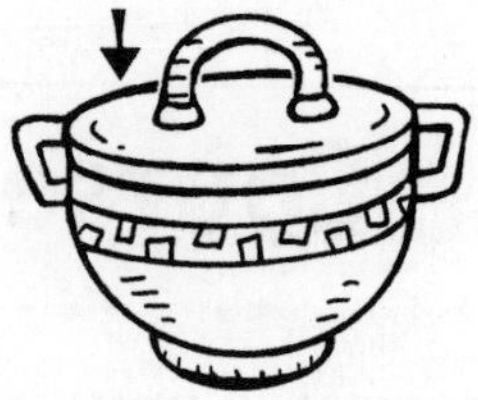   ○ C.

Name _____   Date _____

◎ Cover ◎

The chef put a <u>cover</u> on the pot so the soup would cook faster.

What does <u>cover</u> mean in the sentence?
Fill in the bubble next to your answer.

○ A. a jacket   ○ C. a blanket
○ B. a lid or top   ○ D. a layer

◎ Cover ◎

Write a sentence for each picture.
Use cover to match its meaning in the picture.

1. _____
_____
_____

2. _____
_____
_____

3. _____
_____
_____

◎ Cover ◎

I really like the car shown on the cover of that magazine.

Which sentence uses cover in the same way as the sentence in the box?
Fill in the bubble next to your answer.

○ A. We plan to cover 300 miles on our first day of the trip.

○ B. The wet leaves that cover the path in the woods are very slippery.

○ C. Roger's mother put another cover over him after he fell asleep.

○ D. I paid extra to have my name stamped on the cover of my yearbook.

◎ Guess the Word! ◎

The teacher became _____ when the students wouldn't stop talking.

His dog is a _____ between a German shepherd and a collie.

Choose the word that best completes both sentences.
Fill in the bubble next to your answer.

○ A. mix ○ C. cross
○ B. blend ○ D. trouble

◎ Cross ◎

Mom was <u>cross</u> because Pete walked across the freshly mopped floor.

Which picture shows how <u>cross</u> is used in the sentence?
Fill in the bubble next to your answer.

○ A. ○ B. ○ C.

◎ Cross ◎

Justin's mom told him not to <u>cross</u> the street until he looked both ways.

What does <u>cross</u> mean in the sentence?
Fill in the bubble next to your answer.

○ A. to oppose or go against someone ○ C. to draw a line through something
○ B. to move from one side to another ○ D. to pass while going in different directions

Name _____ Date _____

◎ Cross ◎

> Cross can mean:
>
> A. a symbol used by some churches
>
> B. to go from one side of something to another
>
> C. to mark out or draw a line across something
>
> D. a blending of one plant or animal with another

Find the definition of <u>cross</u> that each person would most likely use.
Write the letter on the line.

_____ 1. editor   _____ 4. student

_____ 2. minister   _____ 5. dog breeder

_____ 3. botanist   _____ 6. pedestrian

- -

Name _____ Date _____

◎ Cross ◎

> Mr. Lim told us to <u>cross</u> out the misspelled words and correct them.

Which sentence uses <u>cross</u> in the same way as the sentence in the box?
Fill in the bubble next to your answer.

◯ A. My job is to <u>cross</u> off the names of people on the list as they arrive.

◯ B. Each time a goat tried to <u>cross</u> the bridge, the troll yelled at it.

◯ C. Sometimes, Jonathan forgets to <u>cross</u> the *t* in his name.

◯ D. I like to <u>cross</u> my legs when I sit on the floor.

◎ Guess the Word! ◎

The geologist will try to _____ the dinosaur bone to find its age.

The two friends made a _____ to meet for dinner.

Choose the word that best completes both sentences.
Fill in the bubble next to your answer.

◯ A. time   ◯ C. age
◯ B. meet   ◯ D. date

◎ Date ◎

Miss Howe asked the class to write the <u>date</u> at the top of their papers.

Which picture shows how <u>date</u> is used in the sentence?
Fill in the bubble next to your answer.

◯ A.    ◯ B.    ◯ C.

◎ Date ◎

By the time Ana's <u>date</u> arrived, it was too late to go to the movie.

What does <u>date</u> mean in the sentence?
Fill in the bubble next to your answer.

◯ A. dark brown fruit that looks like a large raisin

◯ B. to mark with a time, day, or year

◯ C. someone that a person has agreed to meet at a certain time

◯ D. an appointment to meet someone

Name _____   Date _____

◎ Date ◎

Write a sentence for each picture.
Use <u>date</u> to match its meaning in the picture.

1. _____

   _____

   _____

2. _____

   _____

   _____

3. _____

   _____

   _____

Name _____   Date _____

◎ Date ◎

> I helped dad <u>date</u> all the meat before we put it in the freezer.

Which sentence uses <u>date</u> in the same way as the sentence in the box?
Fill in the bubble next to your answer.

○ A. The three girls made a <u>date</u> to meet at the mall on Sunday.

○ B. Omar's <u>date</u> looked beautiful in her long, blue dress.

○ C. I had to sign and <u>date</u> my letter before mailing it to the toy company.

○ D. Bobby took a <u>date</u> out of the box and ate it.

Name ______________________ Date ______________

Guess the Word!

The teacher asked us to __________ a map of our town.

The game ended in a __________ after two hours of overtime.

Choose the word that best completes both sentences.
Fill in the bubble next to your answer.

○ A. tie
○ B. close
○ C. draw
○ D. plan

Name ______________________ Date ______________

Draw

Erika asked if she could draw a picture on the back of her worksheet.

Which picture shows how draw is used in the sentence?
Fill in the bubble next to your answer.

○ A.

○ B.

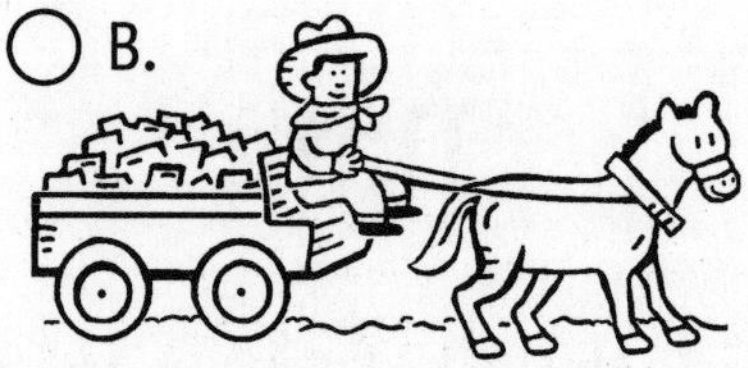

○ C.

Name ______________________ Date ______________

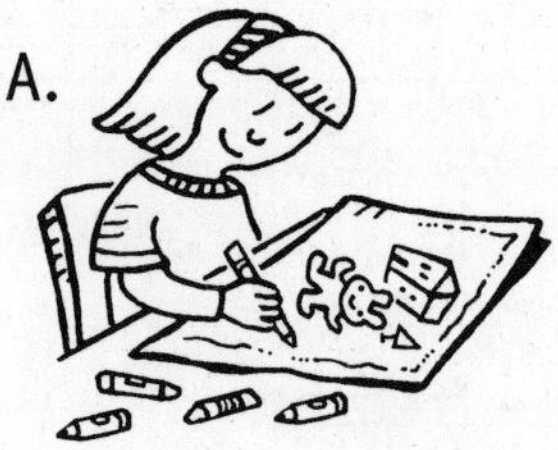

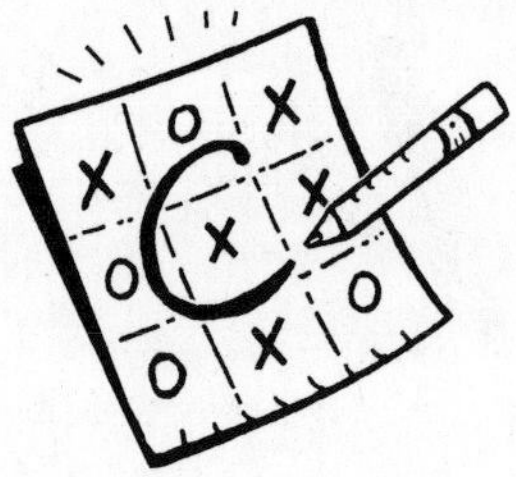

Draw

Every night, I draw the curtains in my room before I put on my pajamas.

What does draw mean in the sentence?
Fill in the bubble next to your answer.

○ A. to make a picture
○ B. to close
○ C. a tie game
○ D. to attract

◎ Draw ◎

Write a sentence for each picture.

Use <u>draw</u> to match its meaning in the picture.

1. _____
   _____
   _____

2. _____
   _____
   _____

3. _____
   _____
   _____

◎ Draw ◎

> Often, my little brother dances around to <u>draw</u> attention to himself.

Which sentence uses <u>draw</u> in the same way as the sentence in the box?

Fill in the bubble next to your answer.

○ A. Sandy had to <u>draw</u> a deep breath before she dove into the water.

○ B. A street clown can <u>draw</u> a large crowd when he performs his act.

○ C. Mario asked his brother, "Did you <u>draw</u> on the wall with crayons?"

○ D. The farmer used two horses to <u>draw</u> the plow across the field.

Name ______________________ Date ______________

Guess the Word!

The chef used powdered sugar to __________ the doughnuts.
Please use this cloth and spray to __________ the furniture.

Choose the word that best completes both sentences.
Fill in the bubble next to your answer.

◯ A. clean
◯ B. dust
◯ C. decorate
◯ D. sprinkle

Name ______________________ Date ______________

Dust

Peter asked the fairy to dust him with her magic flying powder.

Which picture shows how dust is used in the sentence?
Fill in the bubble next to your answer.

◯ A.

◯ B.

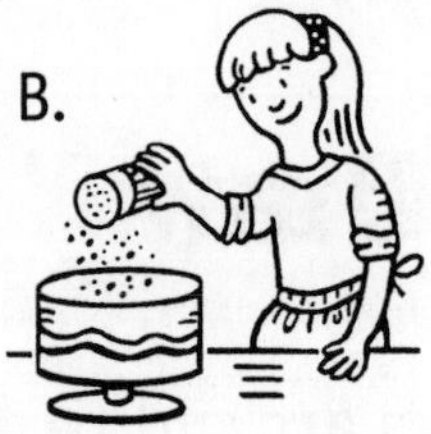

◯ C.

Name ______________________ Date ______________

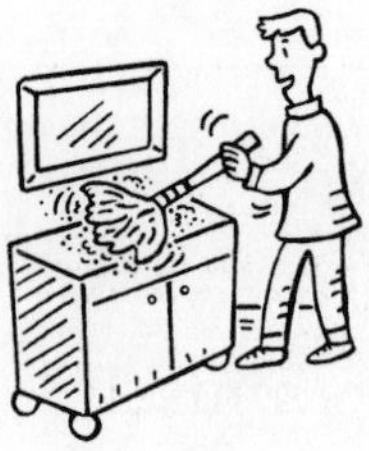

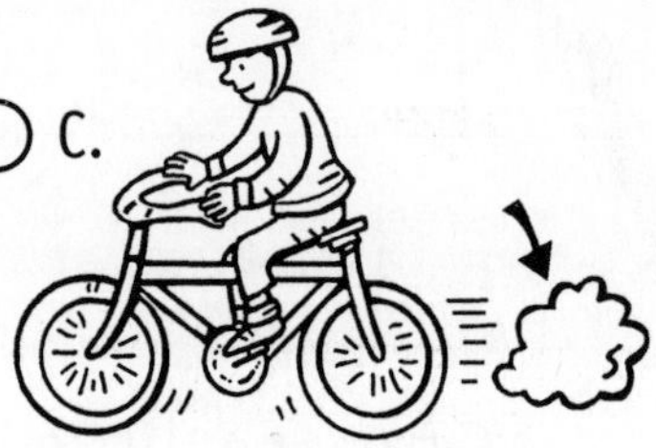

Dust

We had to dust off the chest in the attic before opening it.

What does dust mean in the sentence?
Fill in the bubble next to your answer.

◯ A. tiny pieces of dirt
◯ B. to stir up dirt or particles
◯ C. to cover or sprinkle
◯ D. to remove bits of dirt

◎ Dust ◎

Write a sentence for each picture.
Use <u>dust</u> to match its meaning in the picture.

1. _____
_____
_____

2. _____
_____
_____

3. _____
_____
_____

◎ Dust ◎

> We made a trail of <u>dust</u> when we drove down the dirt road.

Which sentence uses <u>dust</u> in the same way as the sentence in the box?
Fill in the bubble next to your answer.

○ A. I like to <u>dust</u> my toast with a bit of cinnamon powder.

○ B. Emily promised to <u>dust</u> the furniture so it would shine for the party.

○ C. The dog kicked up a cloud of <u>dust</u> as it ran across the dry field.

○ D. The police began to <u>dust</u> for fingerprints at the crime scene.

Name _____ Date _____

◎ Guess the Word! ◎

The referees watched the replay to see if the catch was _____.

The weather was _____ so we decided to have a picnic.

Choose the word that best completes both sentences.
Fill in the bubble next to your answer.

- ○ A. fair
- ○ B. light
- ○ C. nice
- ○ D. legal

Name _____ Date _____

◎ Fair ◎

Mike and Jay ate too many sweets at the county <u>fair</u>.

Which picture shows how <u>fair</u> is used in the sentence?
Fill in the bubble next to your answer.

○ A.   ○ B.    ○ C.

Name _____ Date _____

◎ Fair ◎

Our team has a <u>fair</u> chance of winning the cheerleading contest.

What does <u>fair</u> mean in the sentence?
Fill in the bubble next to your answer.

- ○ A. according to the rules
- ○ B. pretty good or average
- ○ C. a place where products are shown or sold
- ○ D. good-looking

Name _____ **Date** _____

◎ Fair ◎

Write a sentence for each picture.
Use <u>fair</u> to match its meaning in the picture.

1. _____
   _____
   _____

2. _____
   _____
   _____

3. _____
   _____
   _____

Name _____ **Date** _____

◎ Fair ◎

> Owen felt it wasn't <u>fair</u> that his brother went to the game without him.

Which sentence uses <u>fair</u> in the same way as the sentence in the box?
Fill in the bubble next to your answer.

○ A. France holds a <u>fair</u> every year to showcase new movies.

○ B. To be <u>fair</u>, the teacher gave everyone three tries to answer the question.

○ C. My cousin has a <u>fair</u> chance of winning the swimming relay.

○ D. Dad said we would have <u>fair</u> weather for our zoo trip tomorrow.

Name ______________________ Date ______________

Guess the Word!

Grandma began to __________ the fire to keep it burning.
I was a big __________ of *Sesame Street* when I was younger.

Choose the word that best completes both sentences.
Fill in the bubble next to your answer.

○ A. expert ○ C. wave
○ B. blow ○ D. fan

Name ______________________ Date ______________

Fan

Please turn the <u>fan</u> on high until the room cools down.

Which picture shows how <u>fan</u> is used in the sentence?
Fill in the bubble next to your answer.

○ A.

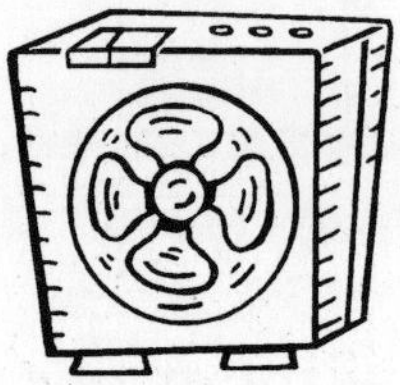

○ B.

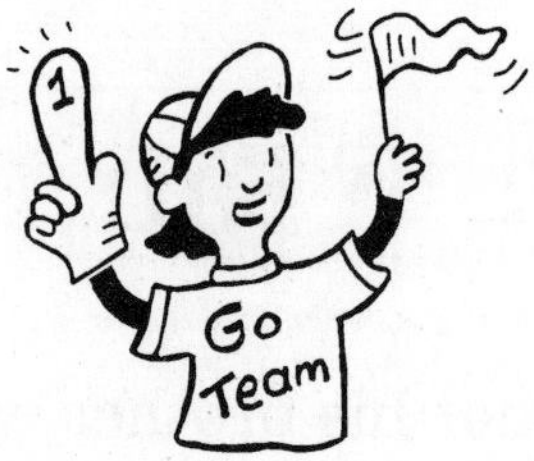

○ C.

Name ______________________ Date ______________

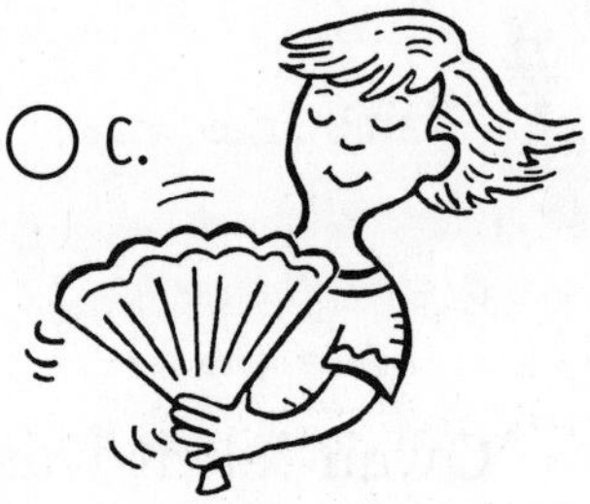

Fan

Searchers began to <u>fan</u> out across the area to look for the lost child.

What does <u>fan</u> mean in the sentence?
Fill in the bubble next to your answer.

○ A. to brush or drive something away with a waving movement
○ B. to spread out from a central point
○ C. to create cool air by waving a piece of paper or other object
○ D. to make a fire stronger by stirring up the air around it

Name _____   Date _____

◎ Fan ◎

Write a sentence for each picture.
Use fan to match its meaning in the picture.

1. _____
   _____
   _____

2. _____
   _____
   _____

3. _____
   _____

Name _____   Date _____

◎ Fan ◎

The people at the outdoor concert waved their hands to fan away the bugs.

Which sentence uses fan in the same way as the sentence in the box?
Fill in the bubble next to your answer.

○ A. We put a fan in the window to blow in the fresh air.

○ B. When I stepped on the mound, ants began to fan out in all directions.

○ C. Mom used a newspaper to fan the smoke away from her face.

○ D. Each student picked up a souvenir fan from the box.

Name ______________________ Date ______________

Guess the Word!

The principal asked each class to walk single __________ down the hall.
Dad keeps all of his receipts in a __________ in his desk drawer.

Choose the word that best completes both sentences.
Fill in the bubble next to your answer.

◯ A. line ◯ C. tool
◯ B. file ◯ D. folder

Name ______________________ Date ______________

File

Joan used a file to fix her broken fingernail.

Which picture shows how file is used in the sentence?
Fill in the bubble next to your answer.

◯ A.

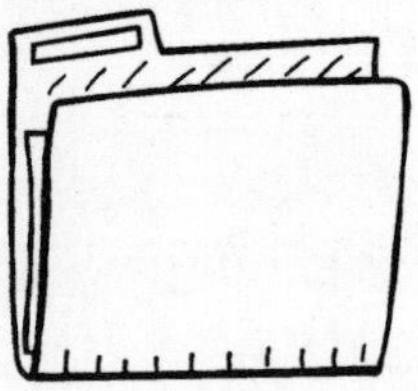

◯ B.

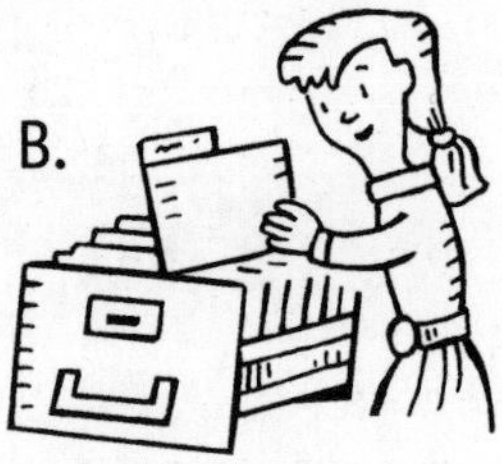

◯ C.

Name ______________________ Date ______________

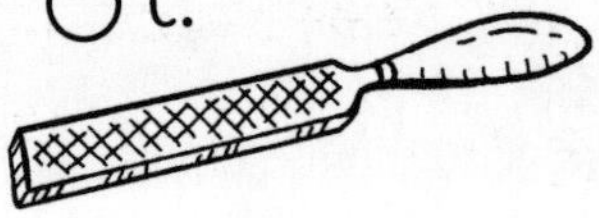

File

Norm went to the police station to file a report about his stolen bike.

What does file mean in the sentence?
Fill in the bubble next to your answer.

◯ A. to line up one thing after another
◯ B. to turn in information to go on an official record
◯ C. to put a set of papers in order
◯ D. to smooth out a rough surface

◎ File ◎

File can mean:

A. to smooth out a rough surface

B. to turn in information to go on an official record

C. data or information stored on a computer

D. a folder used for holding paper

Find the definition of <u>file</u> that each person would most likely use.
Write the letter on the line.

_____ 1. computer instructor   _____ 4. teacher

_____ 2. manicurist   _____ 5. police officer

_____ 3. doctor   _____ 6. carpenter

◎ File ◎

The computer teacher told us to open the <u>file</u> named "Pictures."

Which sentence uses <u>file</u> in the same way as the sentence in the box?
Fill in the bubble next to your answer.

○ A. Lonnie saved his report in a <u>file</u> on his laptop.

○ B. Mr. Day keeps our writing folders in a <u>file</u> cabinet.

○ C. The elephants walked single <u>file</u> into the circus tent.

○ D. The dentist keeps a <u>file</u> on each of her patients.

Name ______________________ Date ______________

Guess the Word!

The van beside us has a __________ tire.

The Ritters live in the only house on our street with a __________ roof.

Choose the word that best completes both sentences.
Fill in the bubble next to your answer.

○ A. smooth
○ B. flat
○ C. dull
○ D. set

Name ______________________ Date ______________

Flat

Ted brought home a flat of tomato plants from the nursery.

Which picture shows how flat is used in the sentence?
Fill in the bubble next to your answer.

○ A.

○ B.

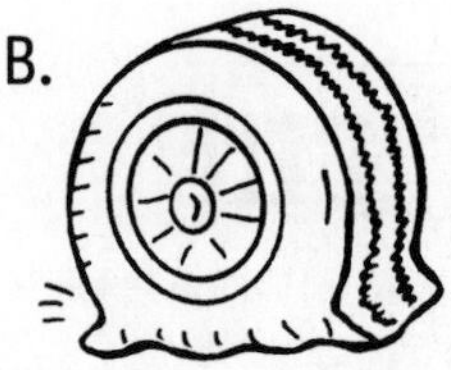

○ C.

Name ______________________ Date ______________

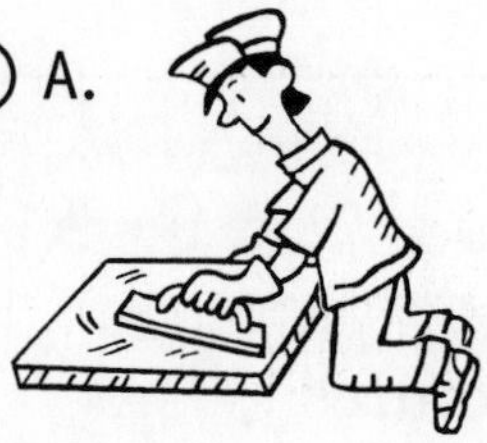

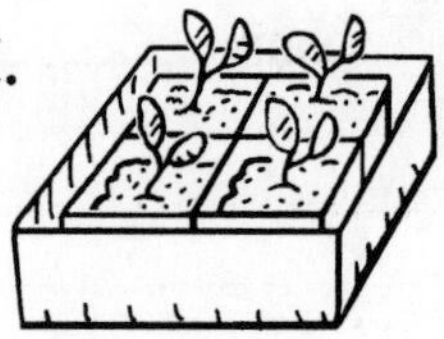

Flat

We rented a flat in London to stay in during our month-long vacation.

What does flat mean in the sentence?
Fill in the bubble next to your answer.

○ A. an apartment
○ B. a tire that has lost most of its air
○ C. a tray of plants
○ D. a shoe with a very low heel

◎ Flat ◎

> Flat can mean:
>
> A. smooth and level
>
> B. lying horizontally at full length
>
> C. a musical note that is lower than the true pitch
>
> D. a tire with very little air in it

Find the definition of <u>flat</u> that each person would most likely use.
Write the letter on the line.

_____ 1. singer

_____ 2. steamroller operator

_____ 3. mechanic

_____ 4. cave explorer

_____ 5. truck driver

_____ 6. band conductor

- -

◎ Flat ◎

> Every time Karl sings a long note, it goes <u>flat</u>.

Which sentence uses <u>flat</u> in the same way as the sentence in the box?
Fill in the bubble next to your answer.

○ A. My sister bought a <u>flat</u> of twelve pansies to plant in her garden.

○ B. He came in first place by finishing the race in seven minutes <u>flat</u>.

○ C. Resa cooks very thin, <u>flat</u> pancakes to make the batter go further.

○ D. My clarinet instructor said that the last note I played was <u>flat</u>.

Name ______________________________ Date ____________________

Guess the Word!

Evan sat at the __________ of the bed to put on his shoes.

Alex broke her __________ when she missed a hurdle during the race.

Choose the word that best completes both sentences.
Fill in the bubble next to your answer.

- ◯ A. foot
- ◯ B. leg
- ◯ C. bottom
- ◯ D. end

Name ______________________________ Date ____________________

Foot

Macy's father built her a dollhouse that stood a foot high.

Which picture shows how foot is used in the sentence?
Fill in the bubble next to your answer.

◯ A.

◯ B.

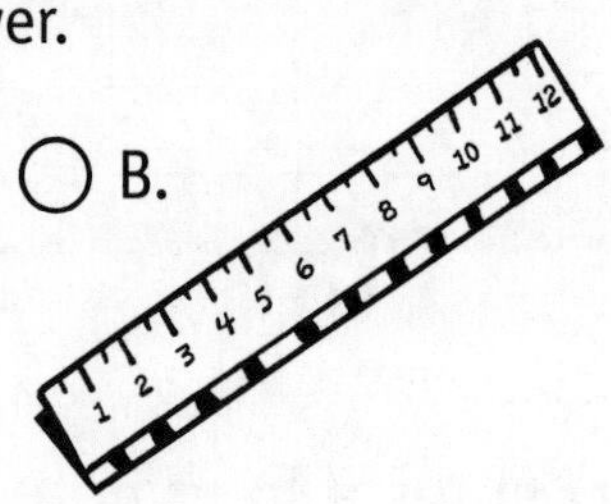

◯ C.

Name ______________________________ Date ____________________

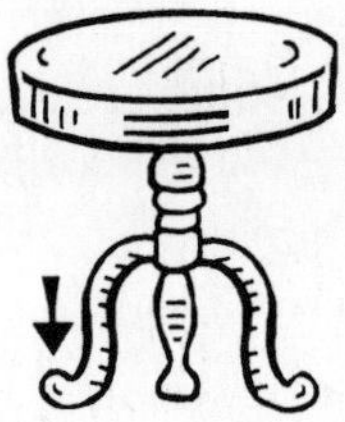

Foot

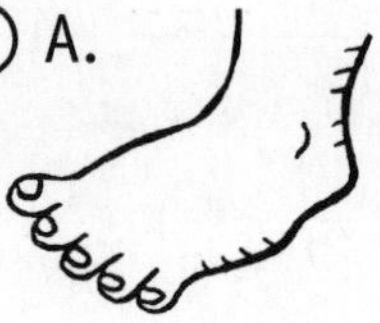

Billy put the blanket at the foot of his bed in case he needed it later.

What does foot mean in the sentence?
Fill in the bubble next to your answer.

- ◯ A. a length covered by 12 inches
- ◯ B. the body part that a person stands and walks on
- ◯ C. the end opposite the head of something
- ◯ D. a way to travel from one place to another

◎ Foot ◎

Write a sentence for each picture.
Use <u>foot</u> to match its meaning in the picture.

1. _____
   _____
   _____

2. _____
   _____
   _____

3. _____
   _____
   _____

- -

◎ Foot ◎

> Our hiking group sat down to rest at the <u>foot</u> of the mountain.

Which sentence uses <u>foot</u> in the same way as the sentence in the box?
Fill in the bubble next to your answer.

○ A. Instead of taking a bus tour, we decided to see the city on <u>foot</u>.

○ B. Nick measured his dad's shoe and learned that it was one <u>foot</u> long.

○ C. Jordan got a blister on his <u>foot</u> from walking all day.

○ D. Tara stood at the <u>foot</u> of the staircase and counted the steps.

Name _____ Date _____

◎ **Guess the Word!** ◎

> An orange and grapefruit have the same _____.
>
> Brooke answered all the questions on the job _____.

Choose the word that best completes both sentences.
Fill in the bubble next to your answer.

◯ A. shape   ◯ C. form
◯ B. paper   ◯ D. body

Name _____ Date _____

◎ **Form** ◎

> The children used mud to <u>form</u> pretend pies and cookies.

Which picture shows how <u>form</u> is used in the sentence?
Fill in the bubble next to your answer.

◯ A.    ◯ B.    ◯ C.

Name _____ Date _____

◎ **Form** ◎

> Three small streams joined together to <u>form</u> a large river.

What does <u>form</u> mean in the sentence?
Fill in the bubble next to your answer.

◯ A. the shape or outline of something   ◯ C. to create something
◯ B. to come up with an idea or plan   ◯ D. to train or teach

Name _____ Date _____

◎ Form ◎

Form can mean:

A. a document with blank spaces for a person to fill in

B. the body or shape of a person or thing

C. to come up with an idea or plan

D. any of the ways a word might be pronounced

Find the definition of <u>form</u> that each person would most likely use.
Write the letter on the line.

_____ 1. fitness instructor   _____ 4. architect

_____ 2. sculptor   _____ 5. receptionist

_____ 3. speech therapist   _____ 6. accountant

Name _____ Date _____

◎ Form ◎

Gabe used a black pen to fill out the <u>form</u> for his passport.

Which sentence uses <u>form</u> in the same way as the sentence in the box?
Fill in the bubble next to your answer.

○ A. After mom signed the <u>form</u>, she put it in the box to enter the contest.

○ B. The roof of the new office building has a very unusual <u>form</u>.

○ C. All the potters in our town <u>form</u> clay vases by hand.

○ D. Researchers are looking for a different <u>form</u> of fuel to use in cars.

Name ______________________________ Date ____________________

Guess the Word!

Every year the fifth __________ classes take a trip to city hall.
This restaurant serves only the finest __________ of meats.

Choose the word that best completes both sentences.
Fill in the bubble next to your answer.

- ◯ A. cut
- ◯ B. level
- ◯ C. score
- ◯ D. grade

Name ______________________________ Date ____________________

Grade

Steve earned the highest <u>grade</u> in our class on the math project.

Which picture shows how <u>grade</u> is used in the sentence?
Fill in the bubble next to your answer.

◯ A.

◯ B.

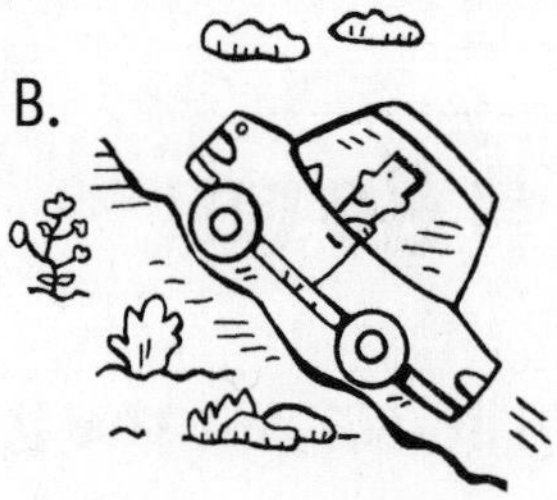

◯ C.

Name ______________________________ Date ____________________

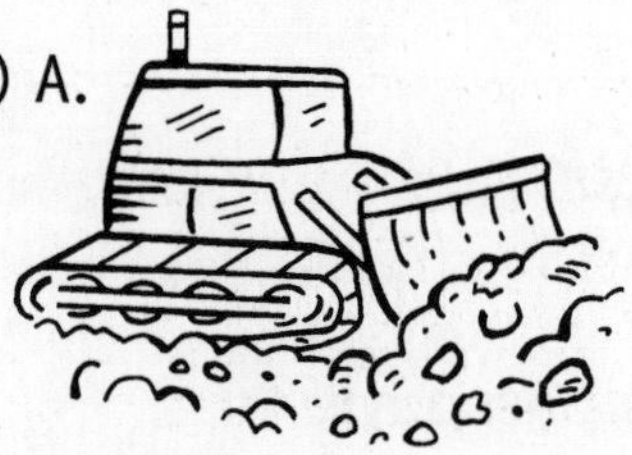

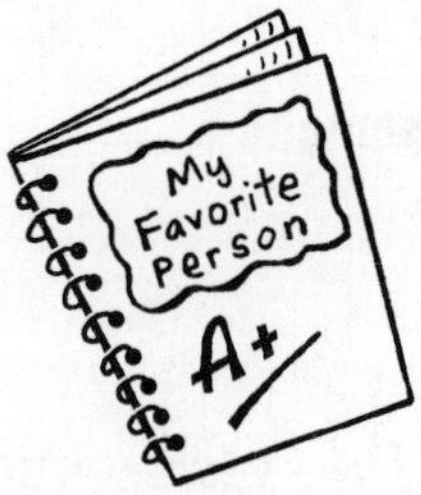

Grade

The steep <u>grade</u> of the trail made it difficult for the hikers to climb.

What does <u>grade</u> mean in the sentence?
Fill in the bubble next to your answer.

- ◯ A. a level or class in school
- ◯ B. a measure of the quality of something
- ◯ C. the score given to a student's work
- ◯ D. the slope of a piece of land

◎ Grade ◎

Grade can mean:

A. to check or give a score to a student's work

B. the slope of land or a road

C. to make something more level

D. a measure of food quality

Find the definition of grade that each person would most likely use.
Write the letter on the line.

_____ 1. truck driver   _____ 4. road construction worker

_____ 2. teacher   _____ 5. grocer

_____ 3. butcher   _____ 6. mountain biker

◎ Grade ◎

Mr. Egan will grade our written plays and how well we perform them.

Which sentence uses grade in the same way as the sentence in the box?
Fill in the bubble next to your answer.

○ A. The Elm Street supermarket sells the highest grade of eggs in town.

○ B. Professor Mills promised to grade our papers tonight.

○ C. We watched the bulldozer grade the lot for our new home.

○ D. Cindy was promoted to the fourth grade at her school.

Name ______________________ Date ______________

Guess the Word!

Mrs. Watson was in a ________ when she locked her keys in the car.

Bud won't eat a peanut butter sandwich unless it has ________ on it, too.

Choose the word that best completes both sentences.
Fill in the bubble next to your answer.

○ A. jam ○ C. mess
○ B. spot ○ D. corner

Name ______________________ Date ______________

Jam

We got stuck in a two-hour jam on the highway this morning.

Which picture shows how jam is used in the sentence?
Fill in the bubble next to your answer.

○ A.

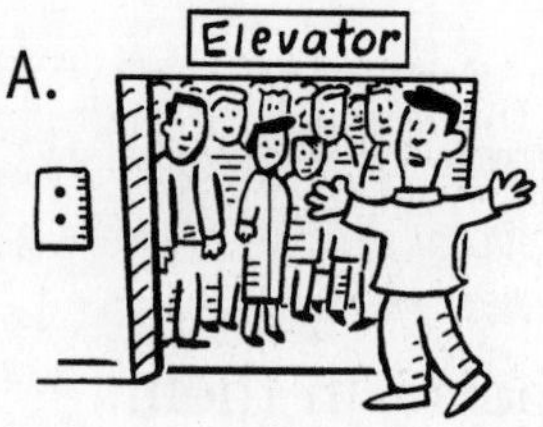

○ B.

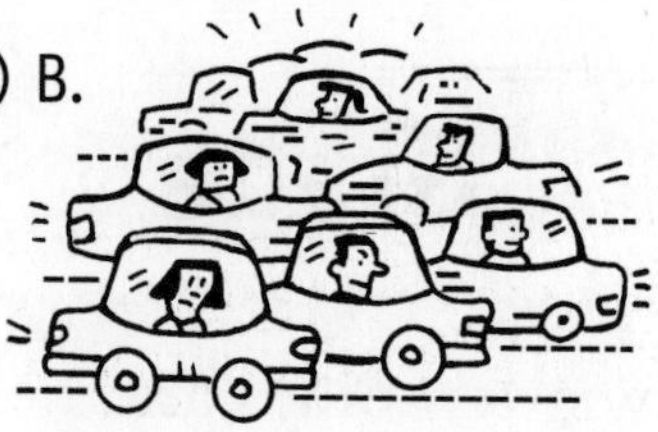

○ C.

Name ______________________ Date ______________

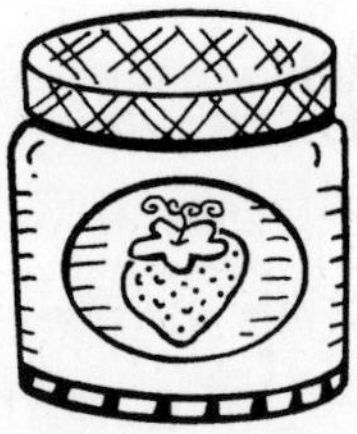

Jam

Beth tried to jam three more books into her stuffed book bag.

What does jam mean in the sentence?
Fill in the bubble next to your answer.

○ A. to force something into a tight space
○ B. to block something completely
○ C. to get stuck or stop working
○ D. to make music

◎ Jam ◎

Write a sentence for each picture.
Use <u>jam</u> to match its meaning in the picture.

1. _____
   _____
   _____

2. _____
   _____
   _____

3. _____
   _____
   _____

◎ Jam ◎

I was afraid the soda machine would <u>jam</u> when I put my money in.

Which sentence uses <u>jam</u> in the same way as the sentence in the box?
Fill in the bubble next to your answer.

○ A. Mr. Hudson had to <u>jam</u> on the brakes to keep from hitting the squirrel.

○ B. Will was in a <u>jam</u> when he missed the last bus to town.

○ C. Do you think this paper will make the printer <u>jam</u>?

○ D. My sister's band gets together to <u>jam</u> in the basement on weekends.

Name _____ Date _____

◎ Guess the Word! ◎

Holly could hardly wait for Mom to _____ the birthday candles.

Dad turned off the _____ to tell us a spooky story.

Choose the word that best completes both sentences.
Fill in the bubble next to your answer.

○ A. light   ○ C. fire
○ B. lamp   ○ D. burn

Name _____ Date _____

◎ Light ◎

The box was so <u>light</u> that Joe thought it was empty.

Which picture shows how <u>light</u> is used in the sentence?
Fill in the bubble next to your answer.

○ A.    ○ B.    ○ C.

Name _____ Date _____

◎ Light ◎

Jenny gave the dog a <u>light</u> pat on the head.

What does <u>light</u> mean in the sentence?
Fill in the bubble next to your answer.

○ A. a pale color   ○ C. a small amount
○ B. soft or gentle   ○ D. very little weight

◎ Light ◎

Write a sentence for each picture.

Use <u>light</u> to match its meaning in the picture.

1. _____
   _____
   _____

2. _____
   _____
   _____

3. _____
   _____
   _____

◎ Light ◎

> Conor painted the sky in his picture a <u>light</u> shade of blue.

Which sentence uses <u>light</u> in the same way as the sentence in the box?
Fill in the bubble next to your answer.

○ A. We waited for <u>light</u> to come so we could see the tracks left by the deer.

○ B. The candle glowed and seemed to <u>light</u> up the entire room.

○ C. I asked Jeff to turn on the <u>light</u> so I could read my book.

○ D. Mary bought the outfit with the <u>light</u> green blouse.

Name _____ Date _____

◎ Guess the Word! ◎

Emma gets the first _____ of the song right every time she sings it.

I keep every _____ that my teacher gives me in a special memory box.

Choose the word that best completes both sentences.
Fill in the bubble next to your answer.

○ A. thought   ○ C. music
○ B. message   ○ D. note

Name _____ Date _____

◎ Note ◎

Dad left a <u>note</u> to remind me to ride the bus today.

Which picture shows how <u>note</u> is used in the sentence?
Fill in the bubble next to your answer.

○ A.  Feed the fish!   ○ B. 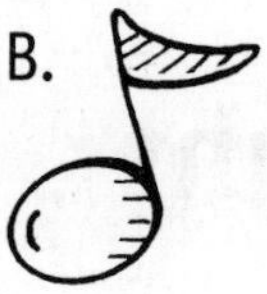   ○ C.

Name _____ Date _____

◎ Note ◎

Mrs. Spell was pleased to <u>note</u> that our class had the best attendance.

What does <u>note</u> mean in the sentence?
Fill in the bubble next to your answer.

○ A. to write down   ○ C. to mention or point out
○ B. to keep in mind   ○ D. to sing

Teaching Vocabulary Words With Multiple Meanings © 2008 by Rebecca Lamb, Scholastic Teaching Resources, 72

Name _____ Date _____

◎ Note ◎

Write a sentence for each picture.

Use <u>note</u> to match its meaning in the picture.

1. _____

_____

_____

2. _____

_____

_____

3. _____

_____

_____

- -

Name _____ Date _____

◎ Note ◎

> Please <u>note</u> how long it takes to finish your homework each night.

Which sentence uses <u>note</u> in the same way as the sentence in the box?

Fill in the bubble next to your answer.

○ A. The <u>note</u> on the refrigerator said that mom was working late tonight.

○ B. A dollar bill is a legal <u>note</u> that can be used to pay for things.

○ C. You may want to <u>note</u> that Alan's birthday is on a Friday this year.

○ D. The band director had us play the <u>note</u> until it sounded right.

Name ____________________ Date ____________

Guess the Word!

The beach is my favorite __________ to go on vacation.
Tina's poodle won second __________ in the dog show.

Choose the word that best completes both sentences.
Fill in the bubble next to your answer.

○ A. spot ○ C. position
○ B. home ○ D. place

Name ____________________ Date ____________

Place

Please place the boxes in the corner by the bookshelf.

Which picture shows how place is used in the sentence?
Fill in the bubble next to your answer.

○ A.

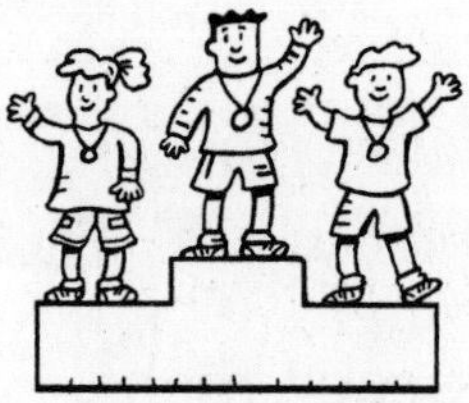

○ B.

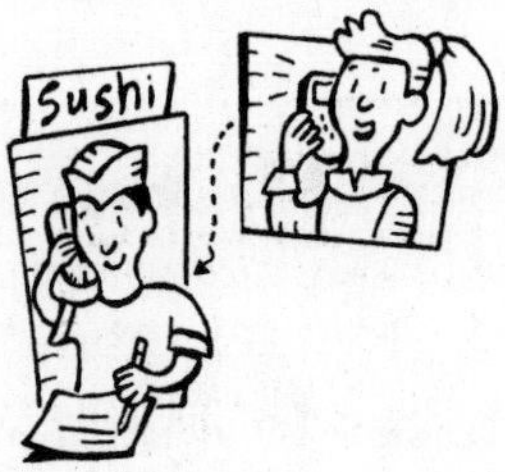

○ C.

Name ____________________ Date ____________

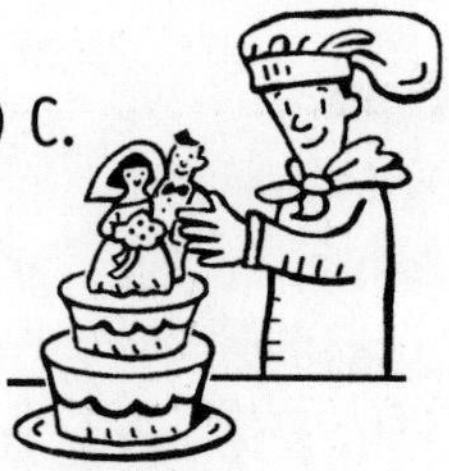

Place

If I were in your place, I would take the lost wallet to the police station.

What does place mean in the sentence?
Fill in the bubble next to your answer.

○ A. location ○ C. rank
○ B. situation ○ D. seat

Name _____ Date _____

◎ Place ◎

Write a sentence for each picture.
Use place to match its meaning in the picture.

1. _____
   _____
   _____

2. _____
   _____
   _____

3. _____
   _____

Name _____ Date _____

◎ Place ◎

> Have you eaten at the new place on Elm Street?

Which sentence uses place in the same way as the sentence in the box?
Fill in the bubble next to your answer.

○ A. We can visit any place in the village that accepts our all-day pass.

○ B. It looks like Diane will place third in the dancing finals.

○ C. Rashad went inside the bakery to place an order for a cake.

○ D. I'll place the keys in this drawer so you'll know where to find them.

Name ______________________ Date ______________

Guess the Word!

Dad took us to see a ____________ at the theater.

Tia left with her friends to go __________ at the park.

Choose the word that best completes both sentences.
Fill in the bubble next to your answer.

◯ A. act ◯ C. play
◯ B. run ◯ D. movie

Name ______________________ Date ______________

Play

The main character in the <u>play</u> enjoys watching soccer games in his spare time.

Which picture shows how <u>play</u> is used in the sentence?
Fill in the bubble next to your answer.

◯ A.

◯ B.

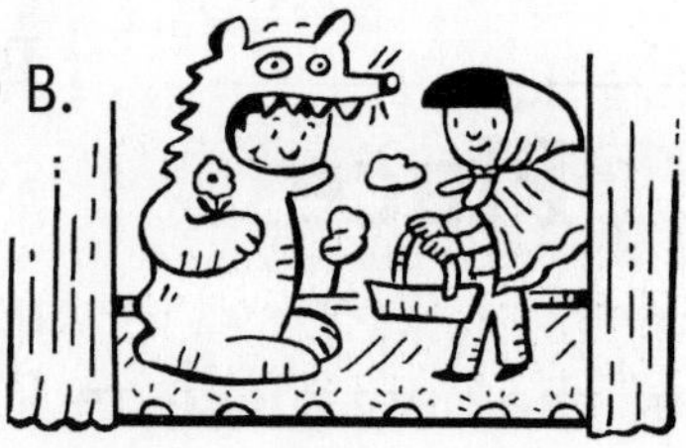

◯ C.

Name ______________________ Date ______________

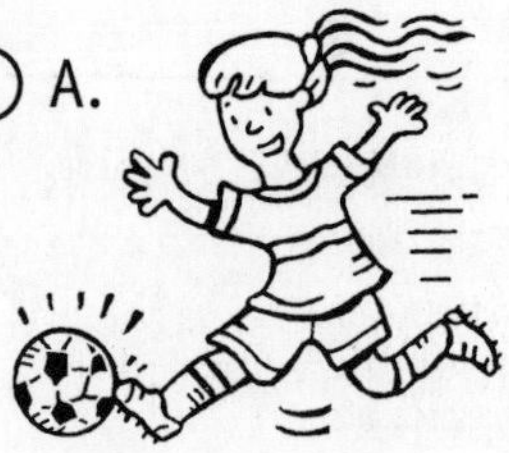

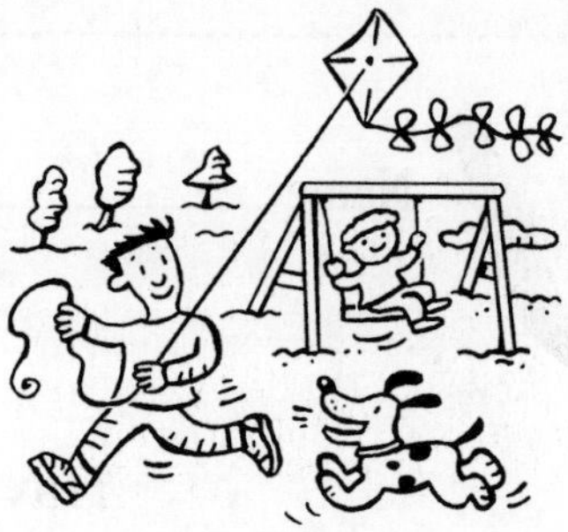

Play

We were surprised at how delicious the <u>play</u> food looked!

What does <u>play</u> mean in the sentence?
Fill in the bubble next to your answer.

◯ A. pretend or not real ◯ C. to make music with an instrument
◯ B. a story performed on stage ◯ D. a move in a game

◎ Play ◎

Write a sentence for each picture.
Use <u>play</u> to match its meaning in the picture.

1. _____
   _____
   _____

2. _____
   _____
   _____

3. _____
   _____
   _____

◎ Play ◎

> My brothers and I <u>play</u> stickball with our neighbors after school.

Which sentence uses <u>play</u> in the same way as the sentence in the box?
Fill in the bubble next to your answer.

○ A. The students asked if they could use puppets in their <u>play</u>.

○ B. My little sister uses <u>play</u> money when she takes pretend shopping trips.

○ C. I'm taking lessons to learn how to <u>play</u> the piano.

○ D. At recess, our teacher likes to <u>play</u> soccer with the class.

Name _____   Date _____

◎ Guess the Word! ◎

I had to _____ five buttons to find the one that lowers the volume.

The newborn kittens _____ against their mother to stay warm.

Choose the word that best completes both sentences.
Fill in the bubble next to your answer.

○ A. crowd   ○ C. cuddle
○ B. press   ○ D. force

Name _____   Date _____

◎ Press ◎

Mrs. Hinton likes to read about her favorite movie star in the <u>press</u>.

Which picture shows how <u>press</u> is used in the sentence?
Fill in the bubble next to your answer.

○ A.    ○ B.    ○ C.

Name _____   Date _____

◎ Press ◎

Tom had to <u>press</u> his pants after he took them out of the clothes basket.

What does <u>press</u> mean in the sentence?
Fill in the bubble next to your answer.

○ A. to iron   ○ C. to push
○ B. to hold close   ○ D. to force

Name _____ Date _____

◎ Press ◎

> Press can mean:
>
> A. to iron wrinkles out of something
>
> B. to push or hold something down
>
> C. to squeeze juice from something
>
> D. newspapers and magazines

Find the definition of press that each person would most likely use.
Write the letter on the line.

_____ 1. elevator operator   _____ 4. politician

_____ 2. reporter   _____ 5. chef

_____ 3. seamstress   _____ 6. dry cleaner

Name _____ Date _____

◎ Press ◎

> Resa tried to press her mom into letting her go to the party.

Which sentence uses press in the same way as the sentence in the box?
Fill in the bubble next to your answer.

○ A. Jason liked to press his cheek against the soft, furry blanket.

○ B. We had to press Kelsey into telling us what was in the box.

○ C. You have to press the red button before you can open the back door.

○ D. The hikers continued to press forward to reach the campsite before dark.

Name ______________________ Date ______________

Guess the Word!

The referee tossed a ________ to see which team got the ball first.
The coach told Sami to rest during the third ________ of the game.

Choose the word that best completes both sentences.
Fill in the bubble next to your answer.

- ○ A. coin
- ○ B. period
- ○ C. quarter
- ○ D. ball

Name ______________________ Date ______________

Quarter

Grandpa will be there to pick you up in a <u>quarter</u> of an hour.

Which picture shows how <u>quarter</u> is used in the sentence?
Fill in the bubble next to your answer.

○ A.

○ B.

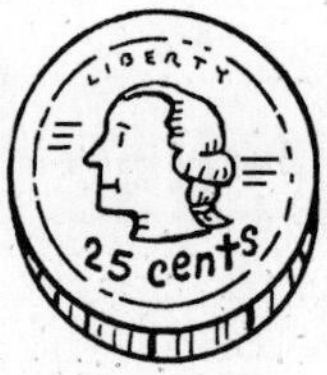

○ C.

Name ______________________ Date ______________

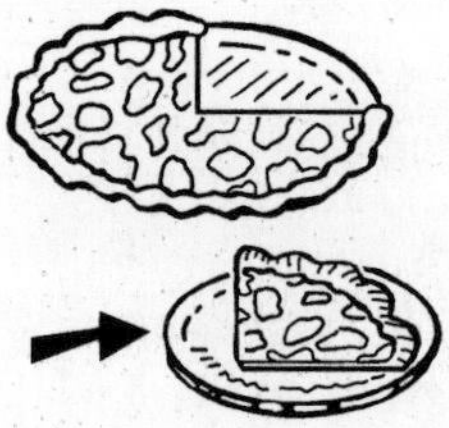

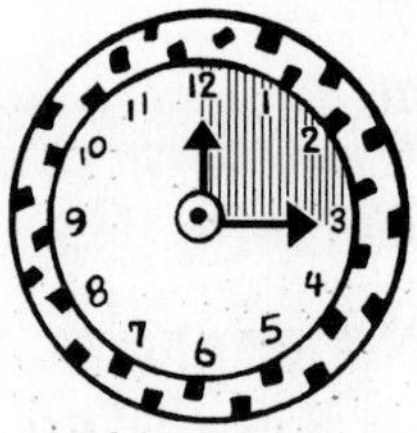

Quarter

I'll look for the lost coin in this <u>quarter</u> of the yard, and you look over there.

What does <u>quarter</u> mean in the sentence?
Fill in the bubble next to your answer.

- ○ A. one-fourth of an hour
- ○ B. area or part
- ○ C. divide into four equal parts
- ○ D. a coin worth 25¢

◎ Quarter ◎

Write a sentence for each picture.
Use quarter to match its meaning in the picture.

1. _____
_____
_____

2. _____
_____
_____

3. _____
_____
_____

◎ Quarter ◎

Each person at the table took a quarter of the giant sub sandwich.

Which sentence uses quarter in the same way as the sentence in the box?
Fill in the bubble next to your answer.

○ A. Liz paid a quarter for each pencil she bought at the school store.

○ B. Grandmother starts making dinner at a quarter past five every day.

○ C. Our teacher said he would quarter the apples to give everyone a piece.

○ D. A quarter of the students in our class missed school on Friday.

Name _____ Date _____

◎ Guess the Word! ◎

Jorge will go to the library _____ after school.

We want to choose the _____ person to lead the committee.

Choose the word that best completes both sentences.
Fill in the bubble next to your answer.

○ A. best   ○ C. right
○ B. straight ○ D. proper

Name _____ Date _____

◎ Right ◎

Steven holds his pencil in his <u>right</u> hand.

Which picture shows how <u>right</u> is used in the sentence?
Fill in the bubble next to your answer.

○ A.   ○ B. 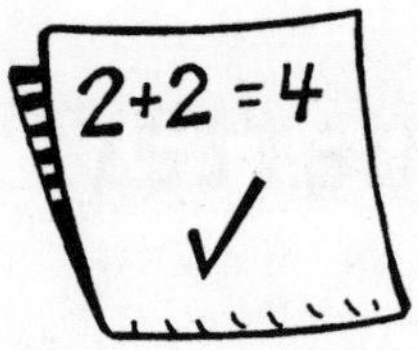   ○ C.

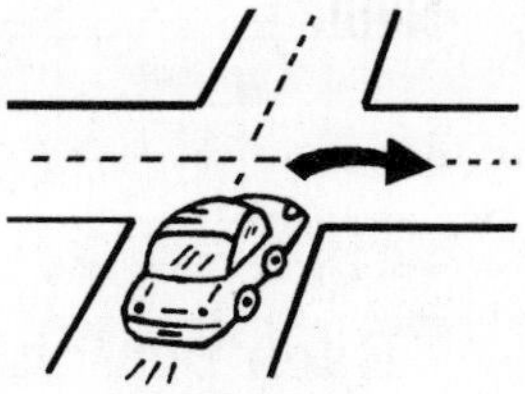

Name _____ Date _____

◎ Right ◎

My head hurts and my stomach doesn't feel <u>right</u>.

What does <u>right</u> mean in the sentence?
Fill in the bubble next to your answer.

○ A. correct   ○ C. immediately
○ B. opposite of left ○ D. well

Name _____   Date _____

◎ Right ◎

Write a sentence for each picture.
Use <u>right</u> to match its meaning in the picture.

1. _____

_____

_____

2. _____

_____

_____

3. _____

_____

_____

Name _____   Date _____

◎ Right ◎

> Caroline gave the <u>right</u> answer to win the spelling contest.

Which sentence uses <u>right</u> in the same way as the sentence in the box?
Fill in the bubble next to your answer.

○ A. Craig chose the <u>right</u> person for the job.

○ B. My little brother puts his shirt on <u>right</u> side out.

○ C. The workers left the bridge <u>right</u> after the rain started.

○ D. Pat made a <u>right</u> turn when the traffic light turned green.

Name _____ Date _____

◎ Guess the Word! ◎

Dean gave Kathy a _____ when he proposed to her.

I let the phone _____ three times before I answered it.

Choose the word that best completes both sentences.
Fill in the bubble next to your answer.

○ A. sound   ○ C. circle
○ B. band   ○ D. ring

Name _____ Date _____

◎ Ring ◎

The bell in the tower at city hall will <u>ring</u> at exactly twelve o'clock.

Which picture shows how <u>ring</u> is used in the sentence?
Fill in the bubble next to your answer.

○ A. 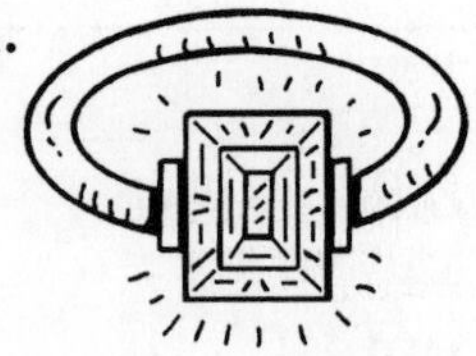   ○ B.    ○ C.

Name _____ Date _____

◎ Ring ◎

The directions said to <u>ring</u> each of my answers on the test.

What does <u>ring</u> mean in the sentence?
Fill in the bubble next to your answer.

○ A. to gather around something
○ B. to make the sound of a bell
○ C. to draw a circle around something
○ D. to call someone on the phone

Name _____   Date _____

◎ Ring ◎

Write a sentence for each picture.
Use <u>ring</u> to match its meaning in the picture.

1. _____
   _____
   _____

2. _____
   _____
   _____

3. _____
   _____
   _____

Name _____   Date _____

◎ Ring ◎

> The two boxers stepped into the <u>ring</u> and shook hands.

Which sentence uses <u>ring</u> in the same way as the sentence in the box?
Fill in the bubble next to your answer.

◯ A. When the bull entered the <u>ring</u>, the first bullfighter ran out of it!

◯ B. Each player received a trophy and <u>ring</u> for winning the championship.

◯ C. Have you heard the morning bell <u>ring</u> yet?

◯ D. Let's <u>ring</u> our flower garden with a circle of rocks.

Name _____ Date _____

☺ Guess the Word! ☺

We saw a raccoon _____ around in our trash last night.

I'm going to the soccer game to _____ for my sister.

Choose the word that best completes both sentences.
Fill in the bubble next to your answer.

○ A. root   ○ C. plant
○ B. cheer   ○ D. dig

Name _____ Date _____

☺ Root ☺

A carrot is actually the <u>root</u> of a plant.

Which picture shows how <u>root</u> is used in the sentence?
Fill in the bubble next to your answer.

○ A.   ○ B.   ○ C. enjoyable

Name _____ Date _____

☺ Root ☺

We went to the debate to <u>root</u> for our school's team.

What does <u>root</u> mean in the sentence?
Fill in the bubble next to your answer.

○ A. to randomly search for something   ○ C. to support or cheer for someone
○ B. to find and get rid of something   ○ D. to make a plant grow

Name _____ **Date** _____

◎ Root ◎

> Root can mean:
>
> A. to cheer loudly
>
> B. the main part of a word
>
> C. the part of a tooth that grows in the gum
>
> D. the part of a plant that grows underground

Find the definition of root that each person would most likely use.
Write the letter on the line.

_____ 1. vegetarian   _____ 4. farmer

_____ 2. cheerleader   _____ 5. football fan

_____ 3. teacher   _____ 6. dentist

- -

Name _____ **Date** _____

◎ Root ◎

> The teacher instructed us to circle the root of each word in the list.

Which sentence uses root in the same way as the sentence in the box?
Fill in the bubble next to your answer.

○ A. George made a dental appointment to have a root canal.

○ B. I can hear my dad root for me every time I come up to bat.

○ C. *Believe* is the root of the word *unbelievable*.

○ D. She tripped over the tree root that had broken through the sidewalk.

Name _____ Date _____

◎ Guess the Word! ◎

A superhero could _____ that high wall easily.

The band warmed up by playing a _____.

Choose the word that best completes both sentences.
Fill in the bubble next to your answer.

○ A. climb   ○ C. note
○ B. scale   ○ D. range

Name _____ Date _____

◎ Scale ◎

Ryan weighed the fish on the <u>scale</u> hanging near the bait cooler.

Which picture shows how <u>scale</u> is used in the sentence?
Fill in the bubble next to your answer.

○ A.    ○ B.    ○ C.

Name _____ Date _____

◎ Scale ◎

We used the <u>scale</u> on the map to see how far apart the two cities were.

What does <u>scale</u> mean in the sentence?
Fill in the bubble next to your answer.

○ A. series of marks used to measure distance   ○ C. a series of musical notes
○ B. an instrument used to find the weight of something   ○ D. a range of values used to grade something

Name _____ **Date** _____

◎ Scale ◎

Scale can mean:

A. an instrument used to find the weight of something

B. one of the thin, flat plates that cover a fish, snake, or lizard

C. a series of marks used to measure distance on a map

D. a series of musical notes

Find the definition of <u>scale</u> that each person would most likely use.
Write the letter on the line.

_____ 1. fisherman   _____ 4. truck driver

_____ 2. car traveler   _____ 5. aquarium attendant

_____ 3. piano player   _____ 6. grocer

Name _____ **Date** _____

◎ Scale ◎

The climbers had to <u>scale</u> a steep cliff to reach the top of the mountain.

Which sentence uses <u>scale</u> in the same way as the sentence in the box?
Fill in the bubble next to your answer.

○ A. Our class observed a lizard <u>scale</u> under the microscope.

○ B. All of Mia's scores are at the top of the grading <u>scale</u>.

○ C. We had to <u>scale</u> the fence because the gate was locked.

○ D. José put three apples on the <u>scale</u> to see how much they weighed.

Name ______________________ Date ______________

Guess the Word!

I'll be ready to go in just a __________.
Sue is __________ in line at the water fountain.

Choose the word that best completes both sentences.
Fill in the bubble next to your answer.

- ◯ A. next
- ◯ B. two
- ◯ C. second
- ◯ D. moment

Name ______________________ Date ______________

Second

Mom took us to the zoo on the second of May.

Which picture shows how second is used in the sentence?
Fill in the bubble next to your answer.

◯ A.

◯ B.

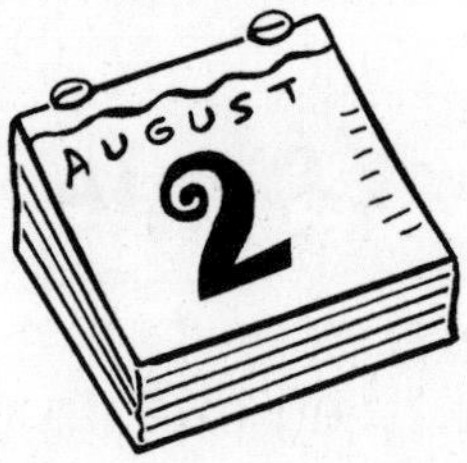

◯ C.

Name ______________________ Date ______________

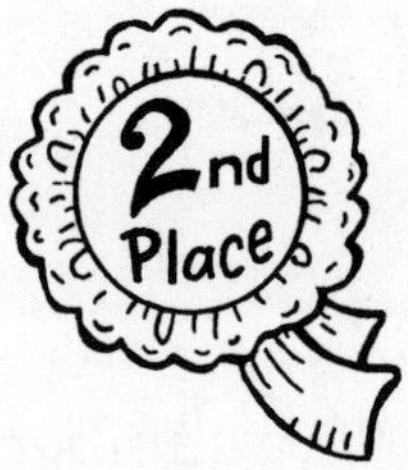

Second

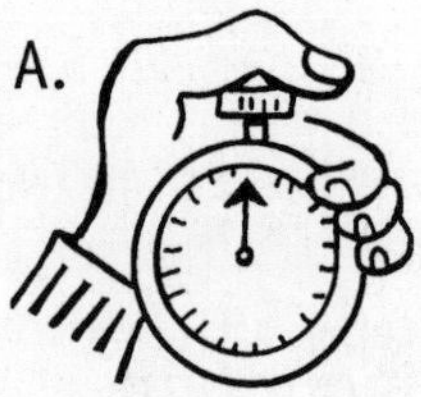

Joel was the second person to ask the teacher that question.

What does second mean in the sentence?
Fill in the bubble next to your answer.

- ◯ A. a very short period of time
- ◯ B. additional
- ◯ C. one sixtieth of a minute
- ◯ D. coming after the first in a series

Name _____   Date _____

◎ Second ◎

Write a sentence for each picture.
Use <u>second</u> to match its meaning in the picture.

1. _____
   _____
   _____

2. _____
   _____
   _____

3. _____
   _____
   _____

- -

Name _____   Date _____

◎ Second ◎

> Lauren asked for a <u>second</u> serving of spaghetti at supper.

Which sentence uses <u>second</u> in the same way as the sentence in the box?
Fill in the bubble next to your answer.

○ A. The teacher asked the <u>second</u> person in line to hold the door open.

○ B. It took only a <u>second</u> for the bee to sting the man and fly off.

○ C. We all <u>second</u> the suggestion to go outside for recess.

○ D. Josh wanted a <u>second</u> opinion about which suit to wear for his interview.

Name ______________________ Date ______________

Guess the Word!

Dara came early to help get the __________ ready for the play.

My parents surprised me with a new __________ of paints and paintbrushes.

Choose the word that best completes both sentences.
Fill in the bubble next to your answer.

○ A. batch ○ C. scenery
○ B. set ○ D. kit

Name ______________________ Date ______________

Set

Henry couldn't find the dice that came with his favorite game <u>set</u>.

Which picture shows how <u>set</u> is used in the sentence?
Fill in the bubble next to your answer.

○ A.

○ B.

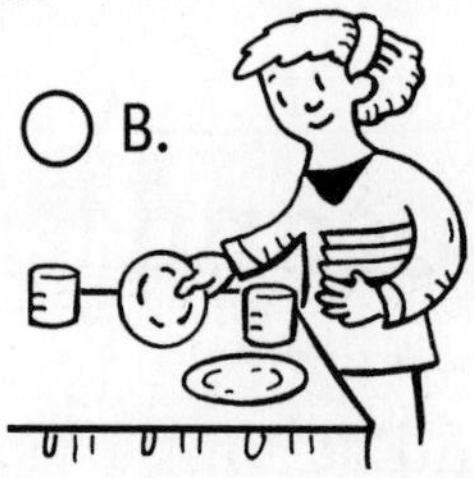

○ C.

Name ______________________ Date ______________

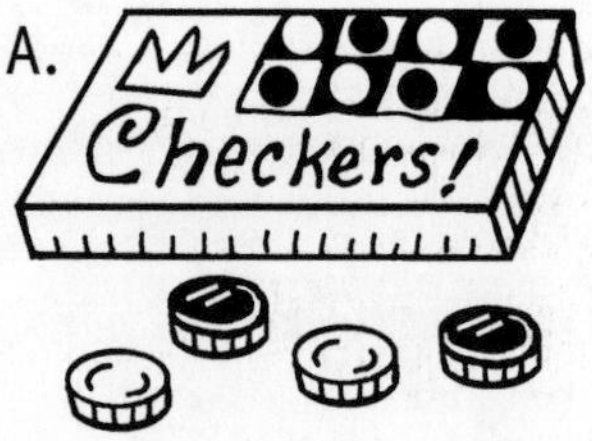

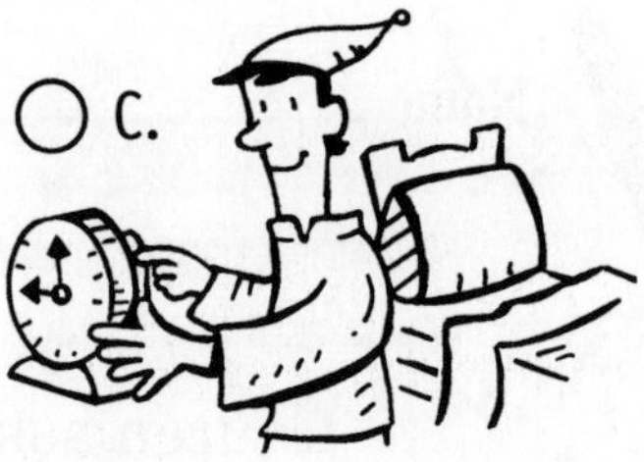

Set

It is my brother's turn to <u>set</u> the table for dinner.

What does <u>set</u> mean in the sentence?
Fill in the bubble next to your answer.

○ A. to put something in a specific place
○ B. to choose a date for a meeting or event
○ C. to prepare a table for a meal
○ D. to decide on something

◎ Set ◎

Write a sentence for each picture.
Use <u>set</u> to match its meaning in the picture.

1. _____
_____
_____

2. _____
_____
_____

3. _____
_____
_____

- -

◎ Set ◎

> We <u>set</u> the date for our class trip to the farmer's market.

Which sentence uses <u>set</u> in the same way as the sentence in the box?
Fill in the bubble next to your answer.

○ A. I'm rested and <u>set</u> to take the math test after lunch today.

○ B. Nate called 911 to report that a fire had been <u>set</u> alongside the road.

○ C. Laura and I <u>set</u> a time to meet to go to the movies.

○ D. Erin added three more dinosaurs to her prehistoric animal <u>set</u>.

Name _____ Date _____

◎ Guess the Word! ◎

Ellie left early to _____ for vegetables at the farmer's market.

Javy's dad owns a small _____ that sells electric train sets.

Choose the word that best completes both sentences.
Fill in the bubble next to your answer.

○ A. hunt   ○ C. pay
○ B. store   ○ D. shop

Name _____ Date _____

◎ Shop ◎

Mrs. Ford loves to <u>shop</u> for new clothes for the holidays.

Which picture shows how <u>shop</u> is used in the sentence?
Fill in the bubble next to your answer.

○ A. FLORIST   ○ B. Car Repairs   ○ C.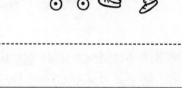

Name _____ Date _____

◎ Shop ◎

Jeremy asked the tow truck driver to take his car to the repair <u>shop</u>.

What does <u>shop</u> mean in the sentence?
Fill in the bubble next to your answer.

○ A. place where things are made or fixed   ○ C. a store where things are sold
○ B. a business   ○ D. a plant or factory

◎ Shop ◎

Write a sentence for each picture.
Use shop to match its meaning in the picture.

1. _____
   _____
   _____

2. _____
   _____
   _____

3. _____
   _____
   _____

Name _____ Date _____

◎ Shop ◎

Aunt Colleen took us to the pet <u>shop</u> to pick out a puppy.

Which sentence uses <u>shop</u> in the same way as the sentence in the box?
Fill in the bubble next to your answer.

○ A. We drove our neighbor to the <u>shop</u> to pick up his car.

○ B. Christopher bought a dozen roses at the flower <u>shop</u>.

○ C. Grandpa went out to his <u>shop</u> to find a wrench.

○ D. I want to <u>shop</u> around to find the best price on a coat.

◎ Guess the Word! ◎

My little sister needs a stool to reach the _____ in the kitchen.

We put objects in the water to see if they would _____ or float.

Choose the word that best completes both sentences.
Fill in the bubble next to your answer.

○ A. sink   ○ C. drop
○ B. fall   ○ D. wreck

- -

◎ Sink ◎

In science class, we learned that pennies <u>sink</u> in water.

Which picture shows how <u>sink</u> is used in the sentence?
Fill in the bubble next to your answer.

○ A.   ○ B.   ○ C.

- -

◎ Sink ◎

Bruce stepped off the sidewalk and felt his feet <u>sink</u> into a puddle of mud.

What does <u>sink</u> mean in the sentence?
Fill in the bubble next to your answer.

○ A. to become less
○ B. to cause something to fail
○ C. to go into deeply
○ D. to become very sad or depressed

◎ Sink ◎

Write a sentence for each picture.
Use sink to match its meaning in the picture.

1. _____
   _____
   _____

2. _____
   _____
   _____

3. _____
   _____

◎ Sink ◎

The old lady watched Snow White sink her teeth into the juicy apple.

Which sentence uses sink in the same way as the sentence in the box?
Fill in the bubble next to your answer.

○ A. Ken left a dirt ring in the sink when he washed his muddy hands.

○ B. Don't let the playful cat sink its claws into your skin!

○ C. The Titanic began to sink after it hit a huge iceberg.

○ D. We enjoy watching the sun sink behind the mountains at sunset.

Name _____ Date _____

◎ Guess the Word! ◎

Walk carefully across the wet floor so you don't _____ and get hurt.

I wrote my name on a _____ of paper and put it in the basket.

Choose the word that best completes both sentences.
Fill in the bubble next to your answer.

○ A. fall   ○ C. slip

○ B. slide   ○ D. pass

Name _____ Date _____

◎ Slip ◎

Can you take this book that's about to <u>slip</u> out of my hands?

Which picture shows how <u>slip</u> is used in the sentence?
Fill in the bubble next to your answer.

○ A.    ○ B.    ○ C.

Name _____ Date _____

◎ Slip ◎

Dad plans to <u>slip</u> out of the room when Mr. Grant's speech is over.

What does <u>slip</u> mean in the sentence?
Fill in the bubble next to your answer.

○ A. to lose your hold on something

○ B. to go or move quickly without being noticed

○ C. to accidentally slide for a short distance

○ D. to make a mistake

◎ Slip ◎

Write a sentence for each picture.
Use <u>slip</u> to match its meaning in the picture.

1. _____
   _____
   _____

2. _____
   _____
   _____

3. _____
   _____
   _____

◎ Slip ◎

Maggie made a <u>slip</u> in her addition and wrote the wrong answer.

Which sentence uses <u>slip</u> in the same way as the sentence in the box?
Fill in the bubble next to your answer.

○ A. Angie bought a new <u>slip</u> to wear under her blue dress.

○ B. Let's tie the string around your finger so the balloon doesn't <u>slip</u> away.

○ C. The hours just seem to <u>slip</u> by when we sit outdoors on the swing.

○ D. I hope I don't <u>slip</u> and give away Mom's birthday surprise.

Name ______________________________ Date ____________________

Guess the Word!

The ketchup left a __________ on Robert's sleeve.
I used binoculars to __________ the robin's nest.

Choose the word that best completes both sentences.
Fill in the bubble next to your answer.

- ◯ A. mark
- ◯ B. place
- ◯ C. locate
- ◯ D. spot

Name ______________________________ Date ____________________

Spot

The guide pointed to a spot on the map to show where we were going.

Which picture shows how spot is used in the sentence?
Fill in the bubble next to your answer.

◯ A.

◯ B.

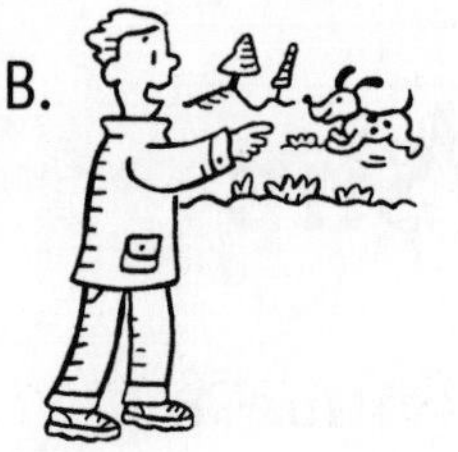

◯ C.

Name ______________________________ Date ____________________

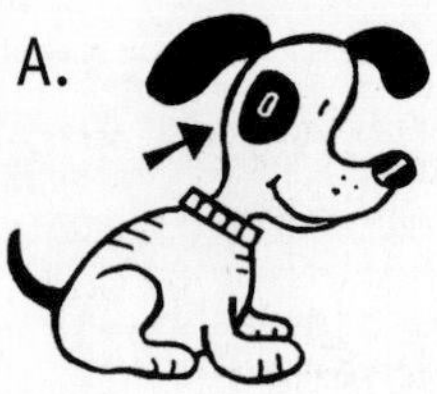

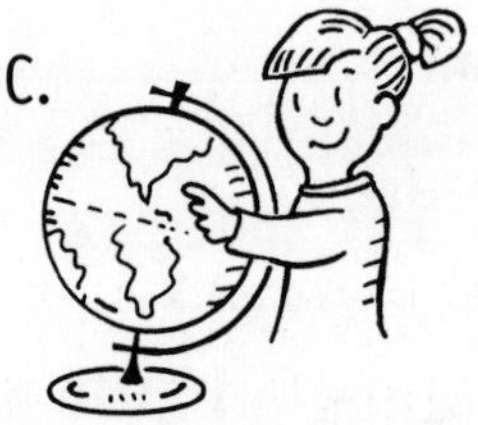

Spot

This is the spot in the story where the boys find the buried treasure.

What does spot mean in the sentence?
Fill in the bubble next to your answer.

- ◯ A. a small mark or stain
- ◯ B. to see or recognize
- ◯ C. a certain place or location
- ◯ D. a position in a list

◎ Spot ◎

Write a sentence for each picture.
Use <u>spot</u> to match its meaning in the picture.

1. _____
   _____
   _____

2. _____
   _____
   _____

3. _____
   _____

◎ Spot ◎

> Ally wants to meet at this same <u>spot</u> at the same time next week.

Which sentence uses <u>spot</u> in the same way as the sentence in the box?
Fill in the bubble next to your answer.

○ A. This is my favorite <u>spot</u> to sit when the teacher reads us a story.

○ B. I noticed that my pants have more than one <u>spot</u> on the left leg.

○ C. Have you been able to <u>spot</u> my sister on the bus yet?

○ D. Barry told me the color of his shirt so I could <u>spot</u> him more easily.

Name ______________________________ Date ____________________

Guess the Word!

Roger spilled his drink on the bottom __________ of the staircase.
The clerk asked the next person in line to __________ up to the counter.

Choose the word that best completes both sentences.
Fill in the bubble next to your answer.

○ A. walk ○ C. move
○ B. step ○ D. rung

Name ______________________________ Date ____________________

Step

Mom and I followed each <u>step</u> carefully to put my new bike together.

Which picture shows how <u>step</u> is used in the sentence?
Fill in the bubble next to your answer.

○ A.

○ B.

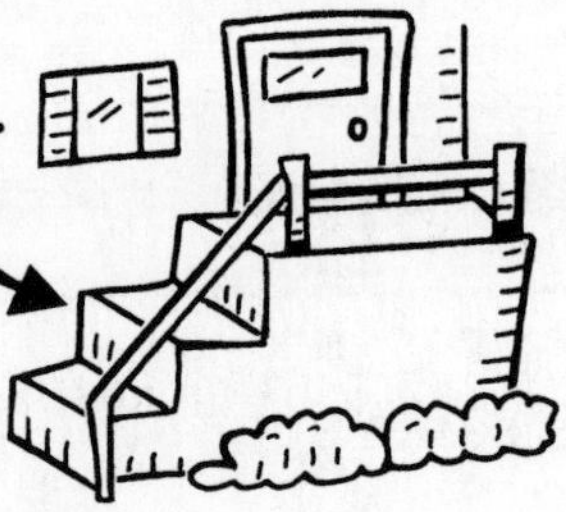

○ C.

Name ______________________________ Date ____________________

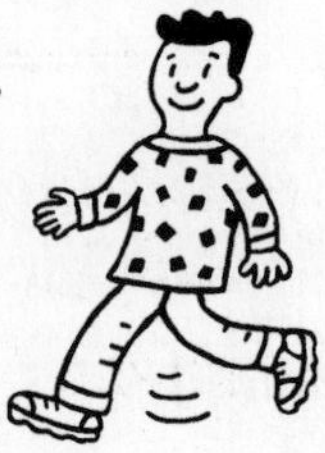

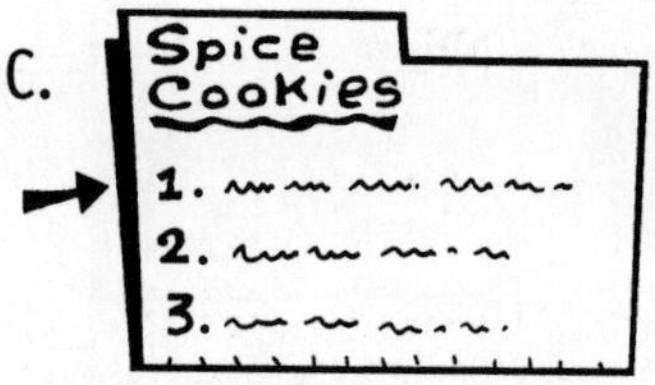

Step

The public library is just a <u>step</u> from our school.

What does <u>step</u> mean in the sentence?
Fill in the bubble next to your answer.

○ A. a short distance
○ B. one part of a set of directions
○ C. one level in a set of stairs
○ D. a movement of the feet in a dance

◎ Step ◎

Write a sentence for each picture.
Use <u>step</u> to match its meaning in the picture.

1. _____
   _____
   _____

2. _____
   _____
   _____

3. _____
   _____

- -

◎ Step ◎

I always wait for the umpire's signal before I <u>step</u> into the batter's box.

Which sentence uses <u>step</u> in the same way as the sentence in the box?
Fill in the bubble next to your answer.

○ A. When we finish, the next <u>step</u> is to put our papers in the red folder.

○ B. I asked Kelly to set my package on the top <u>step</u> of my apartment building.

○ C. Mr. Harris asked for three volunteers to <u>step</u> forward.

○ D. Jude had a hard time keeping in <u>step</u> with the other marchers.

⊚ Guess the Word! ⊚

When she heard the clock _____ midnight, Cinderella ran out the door.

Did you _____ your head on the table when you fell down?

Choose the word that best completes both sentences.
Fill in the bubble next to your answer.

◯ A. find   ◯ C. win
◯ B. hit   ◯ D. strike

⊚ Strike ⊚

If the pitch is called a <u>strike</u>, the inning will be over.

Which picture shows how <u>strike</u> is used in the sentence?
Fill in the bubble next to your answer.

◯ A.   ◯ B.   ◯ C.

⊚ Strike ⊚

The factory workers will <u>strike</u> to try to get safer working conditions.

What does <u>strike</u> mean in the sentence?
Fill in the bubble next to your answer.

◯ A. to protest by refusing to work   ◯ C. to cross out something with a pen
◯ B. to hit something with force   ◯ D. to happen suddenly and cause a lot of damage

Name _____   **Date** _____

◎ Strike ◎

> Strike can mean:
>
> A. to find or discover something suddenly
>
> B. to announce the time by sounding a chime
>
> C. to rub a match to start a fire
>
> D. to swing at and miss a pitched ball

Find the definition of <u>strike</u> that each person would most likely use.
Write the letter on the line.

_____ 1. clock repairman   _____ 4. camper

_____ 2. oil driller   _____ 5. gold miner

_____ 3. umpire   _____ 6. baseball player

Name _____   **Date** _____

◎ Strike ◎

> We watched the barrel roll down the hill and <u>strike</u> a tree in its path.

Which sentence uses <u>strike</u> in the same way as the sentence in the box?
Fill in the bubble next to your answer.

○ A. The <u>strike</u> at the factory lasted three weeks.

○ B. Missy stepped away so that the swing wouldn't <u>strike</u> her in the face.

○ C. Jacob was very excited when he bowled his third <u>strike</u> in a row.

○ D. My uncle hopes to <u>strike</u> it rich by playing the lottery.

Teaching Vocabulary Words With Multiple Meanings © 2008 by Rebecca Lamb, Scholastic Teaching Resources, 105

Name _____ Date _____

☺ Guess the Word! ☺

The quarterback can _____ the ball farther than any other player.

If we test the alarm now, it might _____ our customers into a panic.

Choose the word that best completes both sentences.
Fill in the bubble next to your answer.

○ A. pitch   ○ C. throw
○ B. toss   ○ D. cause

Name _____ Date _____

☺ Throw ☺

Aaron put a <u>throw</u> over his grandmother's feet to keep them warm.

Which picture shows how <u>throw</u> is used in the sentence?
Fill in the bubble next to your answer.

○ A.   ○ B.    ○ C.

Name _____ Date _____

☺ Throw ☺

Kim had to <u>throw</u> on her coat as she ran out the door to catch the bus.

What does <u>throw</u> mean in the sentence?
Fill in the bubble next to your answer.

○ A. to toss something into or through the air   ○ C. to toss something down

○ B. to put on quickly and carelessly   ○ D. to push or force someone suddenly from a seat

Name _____ **Date** _____

◎ Throw ◎

Write a sentence for each picture.
Use <u>throw</u> to match its meaning in the picture.

1. _____
   _____
   _____

2. _____
   _____
   _____

3. _____
   _____
   _____

Name _____ **Date** _____

◎ Throw ◎

Even though he got to <u>throw</u> ten darts at the board, Carlos never scored a point.

Which sentence uses <u>throw</u> in the same way as the sentence in the box?
Fill in the bubble next to your answer.

○ A. Let's hope the nervous horse doesn't <u>throw</u> the jockey during the race.

○ B. Mom is planning to <u>throw</u> a big party to celebrate Dad's new job.

○ C. When I <u>throw</u> the basketball into the air, try to jump up and catch it.

○ D. Miss Hill hopes the new schedule won't <u>throw</u> the class into confusion.

Name ______________________ Date ______________

Guess the Word!

Aunt Martha left a _________ on the table for the waiter.

The coach gives the players a helpful _________ before each game.

Choose the word that best completes both sentences.
Fill in the bubble next to your answer.

◯ A. tip ◯ C. gift
◯ B. point ◯ D. bill

Name ______________________ Date ______________

Tip

Ray caught the glass before it could <u>tip</u> over and spill.

Which picture shows how <u>tip</u> is used in the sentence?
Fill in the bubble next to your answer.

◯ A.

◯ B.

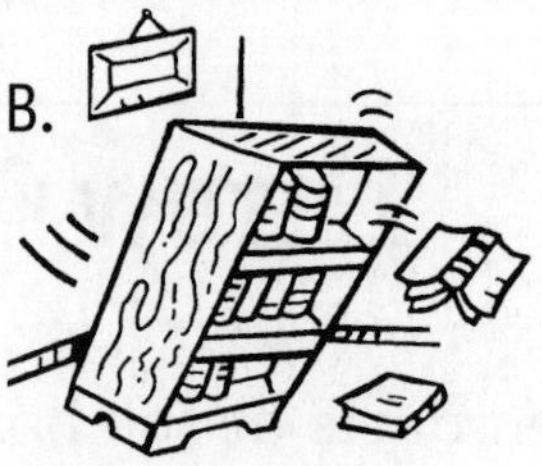

◯ C.

Name ______________________ Date ______________

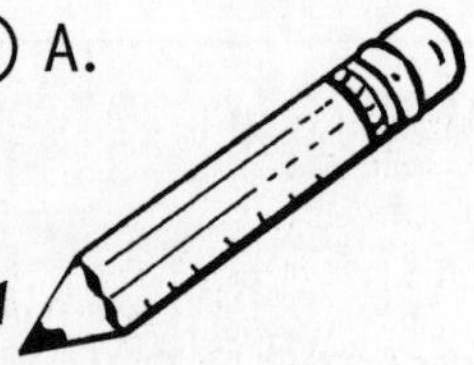

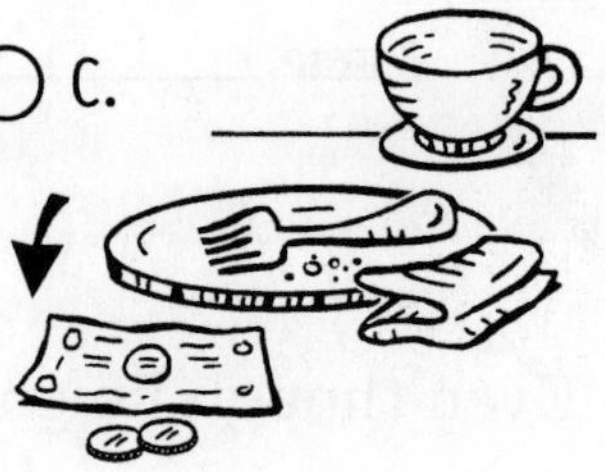

Tip

Marcy poked the lizard with the <u>tip</u> of her stick.

What does <u>tip</u> mean in the sentence?
Fill in the bubble next to your answer.

◯ A. to lean or fall over
◯ B. money given to reward someone for a service
◯ C. the end or point of something
◯ D. a useful bit of advice

Name _____ Date _____

◎ Tip ◎

Write a sentence for each picture.
Use <u>tip</u> to match its meaning in the picture.

1. _____
_____
_____

2. _____
_____
_____

3. _____
_____
_____

Name _____ Date _____

◎ Tip ◎

I gave the taxi driver an extra <u>tip</u> for getting me to my meeting on time.

Which sentence uses <u>tip</u> in the same way as the sentence in the box?
Fill in the bubble next to your answer.

○ A. An eagle nests in a tree near the <u>tip</u> of that mountain.

○ B. Carrie asked to sharpen her pencil because the <u>tip</u> had become dull.

○ C. Sometimes the kittens step into their milk bowl and <u>tip</u> it over.

○ D. Sullivan left a <u>tip</u> for the housekeepers when he checked out of the hotel.

Name _____ Date _____

◎ Guess the Word! ◎

Steven tried for weeks to _____ his dog to roll over.

Mandy was early enough to catch the first _____ to the city.

Choose the word that best completes both sentences.
Fill in the bubble next to your answer.

- ○ A. tail
- ○ B. teach
- ○ C. line
- ○ D. train

Name _____ Date _____

◎ Train ◎

Camille almost tripped when her heel caught the <u>train</u> of her dress.

Which picture shows how <u>train</u> is used in the sentence?
Fill in the bubble next to your answer.

○ A.   ○ B.    ○ C.

Name _____ Date _____

◎ Train ◎

My brother wants to <u>train</u> his bird to do funny tricks.

What does <u>train</u> mean in the sentence?
Fill in the bubble next to your answer.

- ○ A. a line of animals
- ○ B. to teach someone or something how to behave or perform a skill
- ○ C. to cause something to grow in a certain way
- ○ D. to exercise and diet to become skilled in a certain sport

Name _____ **Date** _____

◎ Train ◎

> Train can mean:
>
> A. a line of railroad cars connected to each other
>
> B. to teach someone or something how to behave or perform a skill
>
> C. the back part of a dress that trails along the ground
>
> D. to exercise and diet to become skilled in a certain sport

Find the definition of <u>train</u> that each person would most likely use.
Write the letter on the line.

_____ 1. athlete   _____ 4. bride

_____ 2. conductor   _____ 5. coach

_____ 3. dog handler   _____ 6. dressmaker

Name _____ **Date** _____

◎ Train ◎

> A <u>train</u> of camels carried the tourists across the sandy desert.

Which sentence uses <u>train</u> in the same way as the sentence in the box?
Fill in the bubble next to your answer.

◯ A. To everyone's delight, a <u>train</u> of elephants marched into the circus tent.

◯ B. Mom is trying to <u>train</u> her ivy plant to grow up the garden wall.

◯ C. Jaime wants to <u>train</u> to be an Olympic swimmer.

◯ D. The <u>train</u> on the bride's dress was eight feet long.

Name _____ Date _____

◎ Guess the Word! ◎

This year, I want to _____ all the presents that I give away.

Mr. Moore promised to _____ up the lesson a little early today.

Choose the word that best completes both sentences.
Fill in the bubble next to your answer.

○ A. cover   ○ C. pack
○ B. wrap   ○ D. close

Name _____ Date _____

◎ Wrap ◎

I found an old, small blanket to <u>wrap</u> my new puppy in.

Which picture shows how <u>wrap</u> is used in the sentence?
Fill in the bubble next to your answer.

○ A.   ○ B.    ○ C.

Name _____ Date _____

◎ Wrap ◎

Darrell decided to <u>wrap</u> up our meeting by reading a short poem.

What does <u>wrap</u> mean in the sentence?
Fill in the bubble next to your answer.

○ A. to put paper or material around something   ○ C. to end or conclude an event

○ B. to bundle things into a package   ○ D. to put on warm clothes

Name _____ Date _____

◎ Wrap ◎

Write a sentence for each picture.
Use <u>wrap</u> to match its meaning in the picture.

1. _____
   _____
   _____

2. _____
   _____
   _____

3. _____
   _____
   _____

- -

Name _____ Date _____

◎ Wrap ◎

Please <u>wrap</u> the glasses in paper before packing them into the box.

Which sentence uses <u>wrap</u> in the same way as the sentence in the box?
Fill in the bubble next to your answer.

◯ A. Leo ordered a vegetable <u>wrap</u> and chips for lunch.

◯ B. Bea used the last piece of foil <u>wrap</u> for the baby's gift.

◯ C. Gramps gave Grandma a new <u>wrap</u> for their anniversary.

◯ D. After I wash Spot, I'll <u>wrap</u> him in a big, thick towel.

Dictionary of 50 Words With Multiple Meanings

Act

(noun)
a deed; something that is done
the process of doing something
one of the main divisions of a play, ballet, or opera
a law that has been passed

(verb)
move or take action
to do something; perform an action
to conduct oneself; behave
to perform a role or part (*as in a play or movie*); to pretend

Back

(noun)
the rear part of the human body extending from the neck to the hips
the rear of something; opposite of *front*
the reverse side of something (*the back of the paper*)

(verb)
to move in reverse or backwards
to help or support a person or cause

(adjective)
past or old (*back issues of a magazine*)
located or at the rear of something (*back of the line*)

(adverb)
a return to a former place, time, or condition
in reply or in return (*send the package back*)

Band

(noun)
a strip of rubber, metal, cloth, or other material used
    to tie or hold things together
a plain ring worn on the finger
a stripe of color or material
a range of radio frequencies
a group of people or animals that move and act together
a group of musicians who play together

(verb)
to form or gather in a group
to tie or hold things together

Bank

(noun)
a place of business where people deposit, withdraw, borrow, and
exchange money
a small, strong container for storing coins and other money (*piggy bank*)
a place for storing a reserve supply of something (*food bank*)
a large mound or heap of something
sloping ground along a river or lake

(verb)
to keep money in or have an account with a bank (*I bank with Metro
Savings and Loan*)
to rely or depend on; to be sure of something

Bark

(noun)
the outer covering of a tree's trunk, branches, and roots
the short, gruff sound that a dog, fox, or seal makes
an old word for a large sailing ship

(verb)
to speak loudly or sharply
to make the sound of a bark

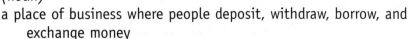

Bat

(noun)
a strong, wooden stick or club used for hitting a ball in certain games
a small, furry animal that flies and is active at night

(verb)
to strike or hit at something
to take a turn at hitting (*as in baseball*)

Bill

(noun)
a statement or a list of charges for goods sold or services or work done
a piece of paper money
a poster or flyer that advertises something
a draft of a law to be presented for approval
the hard part of a bird's mouth; a bird's beak

(verb)
to send a note showing how much is owed for services or work done
to advertise (*We will bill the play as a comedy.*)

Bit
(noun)
a small piece or part of something; a small amount
a short while; a short time
the metal piece of a bridle that goes in a horse's mouth
the part of a drill that makes holes in wood or other materials

(verb)
past tense of bite

Block
(noun)
a plastic or wooden cube that children play with
a hard, solid piece of material with flat surfaces (*a block of wood*)
the length of one side of a street in a town or city
a quantity, collection, or group of things; a batch of things
an obstacle that stops or obstructs the progress or functioning of something
an obstacle that prevents one thing from reaching another

(verb)
to stop or slow down passage through something
to prevent someone or something from reaching a goal (*block the punted football*)

Break
(noun)
an attempt to escape; a rush away from someone of something
a pause or period of rest or relaxation; to stop working for a brief period
an opportunity
an opening made by breaking; a gap

(verb)
to come apart; to separate into pieces
to crack a bone; fracture
to put an end to or stop something
to do better than; surpass (*break a record*)
to enter illegally; to force one's way into a building
to make or become useless because of damage; to ruin
to make known or reveal (*break the news*)

Brush
(noun)
an implement made of bristles or wires fastened to a handle
    and used for grooming, cleaning, or painting
a thick growth of shrubs, bushes, and small trees
a brief encounter or confrontation with something or someone

(verb)
to sweep, scrub, smooth, or paint with a brush
to groom with a brush
to wipe away, remove
to touch lightly in passing

Change

(noun)

money that is returned when the amount paid is
   more than the amount owed
switch, difference, transformation (*the change
   in her behavior was surprising*)
coins ———————————————————————→

(verb)

to make or become different
to replace one thing with another
to exchange, switch, or trade

Charge

(noun)

the price for an item or service; the cost of something
the responsibility, care, or supervision of someone or something

(verb)

to ask a price or fee for goods supplied or a service performed
to put off paying for something until later; to pay with a credit card
to energize or give an electric charge to something (*charge a battery*)
to place the guilt or blame for something on someone
to rush forward or toward someone or something

Check

(noun)

a test or other way of finding out if something is correct or as it should be
a mark used to show that something is correct
a written order directing a bank to pay a certain amount of money ——→
a slip of paper showing what is owed at a restaurant; a bill
a pattern of squares
a ticket, tag, or token given to a person who has left or stored something
   so that the item can be claimed later

(verb)

to test if something is correct or in good condition
to mark with a sign to show that something is correct or has been noted
to look or examine in order to verify something

Course

(noun)

a path over which someone moves
one part of a meal served at one time
a subject one studies in school; a class
an area, route, or track used for certain sports or games
a plan or procedure

Cover

(noun)

something placed on, over, or around something else to protect or hide it

a lid or top

the outer part of a book or magazine

a blanket or quilt

(verb)

to put something over, around, or on top of another thing to protect or hide it, or for warmth

to travel over a distance

to deal with or to address a topic; to investigate or report on an event

Cross

(noun)

a symbol of Christianity

a blending of one plant or animal with another

(verb)

to move or go from one side of something to the other

to mark out or draw a line across or through something

to put or lay one thing across another

to pass someone or something while going in different directions

to go against someone or something; oppose

to breed an animal or plant with one of another kind

(adjective)

angry or annoyed

Date

(noun)

the day, month, or year

an agreement to meet or be with someone at a certain time and place; an appointment

a person with whom one has agreed to meet at a certain time

a sweet fruit that grows on a kind of palm tree and resembles a large raisin

(verb)

to mark something with a time, day, or year

to find out the date of an object or event

Draw

(noun)

a game or contest that ends with an even score (*as in a tie game*)

(verb)

to make a mark or picture with lines; the act of drawing

to move by pulling or dragging; to haul

to direct or attract attention to something; cause to come

to close or shut something (*draw the shades*)

to inhale (*draw a breath*)

to remove something from a container (*draw a name from the bag*)

Dust

(noun)
dry powder made up of tiny pieces of dirt or other material

(verb)
to remove the specks of dirt or dust from something by brushing or wiping
to cover or sprinkle with tiny particles of a material
to stir up dirt or particles

Fair

(noun)
a gathering of amusements and rides for entertainment; a festival
a gathering for a public showing or sell of products; an exhibition,
    display, or market

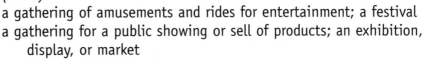

(adjective)
just; not in favor of one over another
according to the rules; not out of bounds (*a fair ball*)
neither too good nor too bad; average
light in color
not cloudy; clear weather
good-looking or attractive

(adverb)
in a just or impartial manner; without cheating

Fan

(noun)
an instrument shaped like a semicircle and waved by hand to stir air
a device with rotating blades and powered by electricity for stirring air
a person with an enthusiastic interest in or admiration for someone
    or something

(verb)
to cause air to move around with or as if with a fan
to brush or drive something away with a waving movement
to spread out from a central point

File

(noun)
a set of papers, cards, or records arranged in order
a folder used for holding paper
a drawer, cabinet, or other container used for arranging and storing papers,
    cards, or records
a collection of information, program instruction, or words stored on a computer
a line of people, animals, or things placed one behind the other
a tool that is used to smooth out rough edges

(verb)
to hand in or put information on record (*to file a complaint or taxes*)
to cut, smooth, or grind
to put a set of papers or documents in order

Flat

(noun)

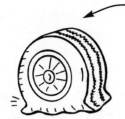

a tire with very little air in it
a tone or musical note that is one half step below the natural pitch
a set of rooms for living; one floor apartment
a box or tray of plants
a shoe with a very low heel

(adjective)
having a smooth, even surface; level
horizontal, lying at full length
wide but not very deep or thick
with very little air in it
below the true pitch in music

(adverb)
exactly, precisely
in a flat position; horizontally

Foot

(noun)
unit of measure equal to 12 inches
end part of the leg that people and animals walk or stand on
lowest or supporting part of something
end opposite the head of something
travel by walking from one place to another

(verb)
to pay for something

Form

(noun)
a document with blanks to be filled in
the shape, structure, or outline of something
kind or type (*light is a form of energy*)
any of the ways a word might be pronounced

(verb)
to make up; constitute
to come or cause something to come into being (*form a plan*)
to shape or develop

Grade

(noun)
a year, level, or class in school
a number or letter showing the score given to a student's work
a measure of the quality of something
the degree to which something slopes (such as a road or land)

(verb)
to check or give a score to a student's work
to make something more level; make less steep

Jam

(noun)
a difficult or awkward situation
a sweet spread made by boiling fruit and sugar together until it is thick
a mass of stopped or slow-moving vehicles that block an area *(traffic jam)*

(verb)
to press, force, or squeeze something into a tight space
to crowd, fill, or block something completely
to become stuck or make unable to work properly
to push something suddenly or hard
to make music

Light

(noun)
a source of illumination, especially a lamp
a source of fire, such as a match or lighter
dawn or daytime

(verb)
to burn or set burning; ignite
to illuminate; to make an area bright with light

(adjective)
pale in color
having little weight; not heavy
soft or gentle; having little force
small in amount

Note

(noun)
a symbol that represents a musical tone
to record or write down information
a short letter or message
a piece of paper money; a dollar bill

(verb)
to observe with care; notice
to mention or point out
to write down or make a written record of something
to keep something in mind

Place

(noun)
a particular location or position
a specific point in a book or passage of text
a particular situation
a certain position in a series *(third place)*

(verb)
to put something in a particular position or location
to give an order for something *(place an order for a take-out meal)*
to rank in a certain position in a sequence *(He will place first in the race.)*

Play

(noun)
a story written and acted out or to be acted out on stage
an activity taken part in for pleasure
a move or action in a game

(verb)
to amuse oneself
to take part in a game
to compete against in a game
to act a dramatic part or role
to act or behave
to perform or do
to make or cause to make sound or music

(adjective)
not real; pretend

Press

(noun)
printed material, especially newspapers and magazines
the people who write printed materials, such as newspapers and magazines

(verb)
to put steady force against something
to push or hold something down
to move forward; go on
to iron an article of clothing; to iron wrinkles out of something
to hug; to hold close
to try to persuade; urge
to squeeze or press a fruit or vegetable to get juice from it

Quarter

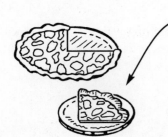

(noun)
any of four equal parts into which something can be divided
one fourth of an hour
a coin worth 25¢
one of the four periods that make up a football or basketball game
one fourth of the time it takes for the moon to revolve around the earth
an area or part of something (*This quarter of the room is for your use;*
    This part of town is called the "French Quarter")

(verb)
to cut or divide into four equal parts

Right

(noun)
something that is correct or true
the side or direction opposite *left* (*turn to the right*)

(adjective)
proper; suitable
true or correct
in good health; well
side or direction opposite of left (*in my right hand*)

(adverb)
in a correct manner; properly
in the exact location or place
immediately; without delay

Ring

(noun)
a circular band often made of gold or silver and worn on a finger
persons or things that are arranged in a circular pattern
an enclosed circular area used for performances or sporting events
the sound that a bell or phone makes

(verb)
to surround with a ring; to encircle or gather around something
to call someone on the phone
to make the sound of a bell

Root

(noun)
the part of a plant that grows underground
the part of a tooth that grows in the gum socket
the main part of a word to which prefixes and suffixes are added
the point of origin or cause of something; source

(verb)
to encourage as if by cheering
to cause a plant to grow roots
to carelessly and randomly search for something
to fix in place by or as if by roots
to find and get rid of something (*root out the problem*)

Scale

(noun)
an instrument used to find the weight of something
one of the thin flat plates that cover the body of a fish, snake, or lizard
a series of marks used to measure distance on a map
a series of musical notes that go up or down in pitch
a range of values used to grade something

(verb)
to climb up or over the top of something (*scale a wall*)

Second

(noun)
a unit of time equal to one sixtieth of a minute
number two in a series
merchandise that has something wrong with it
a very short period of time

(verb)
to support someone or something in their efforts

(adjective)
the next in a series after the first
additional (as in *second serving of potatoes*)

Set

(noun)
a collection of things that belong together
a place or scene constructed for use as part of a play, movie, or TV show

(verb)
to put something in a specific place
to choose a date for a meeting or event (*set a date*)
to prepare a table for a meal
to decide on something (*to set your mind on something*)
to adjust a clock or watch to a certain time
to start a fire

(adjective)
ready or prepared to do something (*We're all set to go on vacation.*)

Shop

(noun)
a place where goods are sold
a place where a particular kind of work is done (*repair shop*)
a business
a plant or factory

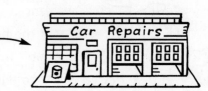

(verb)
to visit stores in order to look at and buy goods

Sink

(noun)
a bowl or basin used to hold water for washing

(verb)
to go down or cause to go down
to fall into a certain state; to become very sad or depressed
to go into deeply (*Sink your teeth into this juicy apple.*)
to cause something to fail
to become less (*as in value, amount, or quality*)

Slip

(noun)
a type of ladies' underwear worn under a dress or skirt
a small piece of paper
a careless mistake

(verb)
to accidentally slide for a short distance
to fall down
to accidentally slide or move out of place or from someone's grasp
to go or move quickly without being noticed
to escape or get loose from something
to make a mistake

Spot

(noun)
a roundish mark or area that is different from the area around it; a stain
a certain place or location
a position in a list (*She's in the first spot to sing for the judges.*)

(verb)
to see or notice someone or something that one has been looking for
to mark or cause to be marked with spots

Step

(noun)
the movement of placing one foot in front of the other when walking
    or running
one level in a set of stairs
a short distance
one part of a set of directions
a movement of the feet in a dance

(verb)
to pick up and put down one foot after another; to walk

Strike

(noun)
a refusal to work, or a walkout, as a form of protest
a perfectly pitched ball (*The pitcher threw a strike.*)

(verb)
to hit something with force
to protest by refusing to work
to swing at and miss a correctly pitched ball
to find or discover something suddenly (*such as gold or oil*)
to remove, cancel, or cross out something (*as with a pen*)
to set something on fire by rubbing one thing against another (*strike a match*)
to happen suddenly and/or to cause harm or damage (*Did lightning strike the tower?*)
to announce the time by sounding a chime
to give a certain impression (*You strike me as courageous.*)

Throw

(noun)
a light blanket or covering used on furniture

(verb)
to toss or send something up into or through the air
to toss or make something fall to the ground
to quickly and carelessly put something somewhere
to put clothing on quickly and carelessly
to put something on or together quickly and carelessly
to cause someone or something to suddenly enter in a certain condition
    (*throw into a panic*)
to push or force someone suddenly from a seat

Tip

(noun)
the end part or point of something
an extra sum of money that is given to thank someone for good service
a useful piece of information

(verb)
to tilt; to raise one end of something
to knock or turn over
to give someone extra money for providing good service (*tip the waiter*)

Train

(noun)
a line of railroad cars connected together
a group of people, animals, or vehicles traveling together in
    a long line
back part of a dress that trails along the ground behind the
    person who wears it

(verb)
to teach someone or something how to behave or perform a skill
to exercise and diet to become skilled in a certain sport
to cause something to grow in a certain way (*such as a plant*)

Wrap

(noun)
paper or a soft material used to enclose something or someone
a sandwich in which the filling is rolled into a tortilla
an article of clothing made of soft material which is draped around
    the body

(verb)
to cover or enclose something in paper or a soft material
to end or conclude an event

⊚ Answers ⊚

Act
page 14
top: B
middle: A
bottom: A

page 15
top: Answers will vary.
Check sentences for
correct use of the word
meaning.
bottom: C

Back
page 16
top: A
middle: B
bottom: C

page 17
top: Answers will vary.
Check sentences for
correct use of the word
meaning.
bottom: D

Band
page 18
top: C
middle: C
bottom: A

page 19
top: Answers will vary.
Check sentences for
correct use of the word
meaning.
bottom: D

Bank
page 20
top: D
middle: B
bottom: C

page 21
top: 1. D, 2. C, 3. B,
4. A, 5. B, 6. C
bottom: A

Bark
page 22
top: C
middle: B
bottom: A

page 23
top: 1. B, 2. D, 3. A,
4. B, 5. C, 6. D
bottom: D

Bat
page 24
top: A
middle: C
bottom: C

page 25
top: Answers will vary.
Check sentences for
correct use of the word
meaning.
bottom: C

Bill
page 26
top: C
middle: A
bottom: D

page 27
top: 1. C, 2. D, 3. A,
4. B., 5. C., 6. A
bottom: B

Bit
page 28
top: D
middle: C
bottom: B

page 29
top: Answers will vary.
Check sentences for
correct use of the word
meaning.
bottom: D

Block
page 30
top: C
middle: A
bottom: D

page 31
top: Answers will vary.
Check sentences for
correct use of the word
meaning.
bottom: C

Break
page 32
top: B
middle: A
bottom: B

page 33
top: Answers will vary.
Check sentences for
correct use of the word
meaning.
bottom: D

Brush
page 34
top: A
middle: C
bottom: B

page 35
top: Answers will vary.
Check sentences for
correct use of the word
meaning.
bottom: B

Change
page 36
top: C
middle: C
bottom: B

page 37
top: Answers will vary.
Check sentences for
correct use of the word
meaning.
bottom: A

Charge
page 38
top: D
middle: C
bottom: A

page 39
top: Answers will vary.
Check sentences for
correct use of the word
meaning.
bottom: C

Check
page 40
top: A
middle: B
bottom: A

page 41
top: 1. D, 2. A, 3. C,
4. B, 5. A, 6. B
bottom: D

Course
page 42
top: A
middle: B
bottom: D

page 43
top: 1. B, 2. D, 3. A,
4. B, 5. A, 6. C
bottom: C

Cover
page 44
top: B
middle: A
bottom: B

page 45
top: Answers will vary.
Check sentences for
correct use of the word
meaning.
bottom: D

Cross
page 46
top: C
middle: A
bottom: B

page 47
top: 1. C, 2. A, 3. D,
4. C, 5. D, 6. B
bottom: A

Date
page 48
top: D
middle: B
bottom: C

page 49
top: Answers will vary.
Check sentences for
correct use of the word
meaning.
bottom: C

Draw
page 50
top: C
middle: A
bottom: B

page 51
top: Answers will vary.
Check sentences for
correct use of the word
meaning.
bottom: B

Dust
page 52
top: B
middle: B
bottom: D

page 53
top: Answers will vary.
Check sentences for
correct use of the word
meaning.
bottom: C

Fair
page 54
top: A
middle: C
bottom: B

page 55
top: Answers will vary.
Check sentences for
correct use of the word
meaning.
bottom: B

Fan
page 56
top: D
middle: A
bottom: B

Cross
page 57
top: Answers will vary.
Check sentences for
correct use of the word
meaning.
bottom: C

File
page 58
top: B
middle: C
bottom: B

page 59
top: 1. C, 2. A, 3. D,
4. D, 5. B, 6. A
bottom: A

Flat
page 60
top: B
middle: C
bottom: A

page 61
top: 1. C, 2. A, 3. D,
4. B, 5. D, 6. C
bottom: D

Foot
page 62
top: A
middle: B
bottom: C

page 63
top: Answers will vary.
Check sentences for
correct use of the word
meaning.
bottom: D

Form
page 64
top: C
middle: B
bottom: C

page 65
top: 1. B, 2. B, 3. D,
4. C. 5. A, 6. A
bottom: A

Grade
page 66
top: D
middle: C
bottom: D

page 67
top: 1. B, 2. A, 3. D,
4. C, 5. D, 6. B
bottom: B

Jam
page 68
top: A
middle: B
bottom: A

page 69
top: Answers will vary.
Check sentences for
correct use of the word
meaning.
bottom: C

Light
page 70
top: A
middle: C
bottom: B

page 71
top: Answers will vary.
Check sentences for
correct use of the word
meaning.
bottom: D

Note
page 72
top: D
middle: A
bottom: C

page 73
top: Answers will vary.
Check sentences for
correct use of the word
meaning.
bottom: C

Place
page 74
top: D
middle: C
bottom: B

page 75
top: Answers will vary.
Check sentences for
correct use of the word
meaning.
bottom: A

Play
page 76
top: C
middle: B
bottom: A

page 77
top: Answers will vary.
Check sentences for
correct use of the word
meaning.
bottom: D

Press
page 78
top: B
middle: A
bottom: A

page 79
top: 1. B, 2. D, 3. A,
4. D, 5. C, 6. A
bottom: B

Quarter
page 80
top: C
middle: C
bottom: B

page 81
top: Answers will vary.
Check sentences for
correct use of the word
meaning.
bottom: D

Right
page 82
top: C
middle: A
bottom: D

page 83
top: Answers will vary.
Check sentences for
correct use of the word
meaning.
bottom: A

Ring
page 84
top: D
middle: B
bottom: C

page 85
top: Answers will vary.
Check sentences for
correct use of the word
meaning.
bottom: A

Root
page 86
top: A
middle: A
bottom: C

page 87
top: 1. D, 2. A, 3. B,
4. D, 5. A, 6. C
bottom: C

Scale
page 88
top: B
middle: C
bottom: A

page 89
top: 1. B, 2. C, 3. D,
4. C, 5. B, 6. A
bottom: C

Second
page 90
top: C
middle: B
bottom: D

page 91
top: Answers will vary.
Check sentences for
correct use of the word
meaning.
bottom: D

Set
page 92
top: B
middle: A
bottom: C

page 93
top: Answers will vary.
Check sentences for
correct use of the word
meaning.
bottom: C

Shop
page 94
top: D
middle: C
bottom: A

page 95
top: Answers will vary.
Check sentences for
correct use of the word
meaning.
bottom: B

Sink
page 96
top: A
middle: C
bottom: C

page 97
top: Answers will vary.
Check sentences for
correct use of the word
meaning.
bottom: B

Slip
page 98
top: C
middle: A
bottom: B

page 99
top: Answers will vary.
Check sentences for
correct use of the word
meaning.
bottom: D

Spot
page 100
top: D
middle: C
bottom: C

page 101
top: Answers will vary.
Check sentences for
correct use of the word
meaning.
bottom: A

Step
page 102
top: B
middle: C
bottom: A

page 103
top: Answers will vary.
Check sentences for
correct use of the word
meaning.
bottom: C

Strike
page 104
top: D
middle: B
bottom: A

page 105
top: 1. B, 2. A, 3. D,
4. C, 5. A, 6. D
bottom: B

Throw
page 106
top: C
middle: A
bottom: B

page 107
top: Answers will vary.
Check sentences for
correct use of the word
meaning.
bottom: C

Tip
page 108
top: A
middle: B
bottom: C

page 109
top: Answers will vary.
Check sentences for
correct use of the word
meaning.
bottom: D

Train
page 110
top: D
middle: C
bottom: B

page 111
top: 1. D, 2. A, 3. B,
4. C, 5. B, 6. C
bottom: A

Wrap
page 112
top: B
middle: B
bottom: C

page 113
top: Answers will vary.
Check sentences for
correct use of the word
meaning.
bottom: D